HARD AGROUND

with Eddie Jones

Hard Aground
with Eddie Jones

Inspiration for the Navigationally Challenged

**The collected columns of
Coastal Cruising's
best-known curmudgeon**

Eddie Jones

Slip None Writers Guild
Oriental, North Carolina

Hard Aground with Eddie Jones
The collected columns of Coastal Cruising's best-known curmudgeon

All Rights Reserved © 2003 by Eddie Jones

Visit the author online at: www.eddiejones.org

Published by
Slip None Writers Guild
Oriental, NC 28571

Do not try this at home. Your boat probably won't fit in the living room.

ISBN: 978-0-982-20650-8

Printed in the United States of America
3nd Printing - 2009

1. Humor - American   2. Boating – North Carolina

www.hardaground.com

This book is dedicated to all my friends in Oriental who have, over the years, cheered and jeered my mis-adventures including, but not limited to; Danny, Bill, Linda, Simon, Buck, Dave, Ralph, Wally, Sue, Knute, Sonny, Barb, Bob, Peter, Jay, Bert and, of course, John Farmer at Camp Don Lee who allowed me to park my boat on top of his canoe dock.—EJ

"The first rule of navigation is never drive the boat where the birds are walking."
—Travis McGee

Contents

I had the good fortune to become a regular reader of Hard Aground with Eddie during his years as a columnist for *Carolina Cruising Magazine*. Eddie's extraordinary talent as a nautical writer grew with each issue and eventually his column became one of the most popular features of the magazine. (I like to think my Carolina cruising guides were THE most popular feature. ☺)

I deeply commend the various Hard Aground columns collected in this book to my fellow cruisers. Perusing these pages will, I have no doubt, make your time on the water, or even your time in the armchair, a happier and far richer experience. All of us who participate in the cruising lifestyle can be very thankful that Eddie has "sounded" the shoals and sandbars of the Carolina coast to such an extent that no further coastal exploration of submerged islands is necessary.

All that is required is to read and heed his tales of woe and be grateful it is Eddie who is Hard Aground and not you or I!

—Claiborne S. Young

Moments Frozen in Time

"The cockroach has the same chemical dependency to junk food as a teenage boy and will eat anything left on a boat, including a small child, if it is left unwrapped. Packaging doesn't discourage the juvenile male and this is the principle difference between a cockroach and my boys."

RETIREMENT ACT NOW!

If you're skimping and saving for your retirement, with hopes of spending winters in the Keys and summers in New England, exploring turquoise harbors and pristine beaches, you'd better think again. Retirement as we know it may be fading as fast as crushed ice in a warm Margarita. Sociologists warn us that by the year 2000, one-third of the population will be over the age of 60 and rushing toward retirement. That, my friend, is a coastal cruiser's nightmare. Imagine 100 million people clogging the waterways and harbors with slow boats and short tempers and you have a pretty good idea of where we're headed. Worse still, the government predicts the dwindling labor force will be unable to support an already strained retirement fund. As a matter of simple survival, many of us will be forced to work into and through our golden years just to make ends meet, because it is a sure bet our children won't take care of us. If Junior couldn't be trusted to take care of the dog, you better believe he won't do much better by us.

Retirement at 65, ha! Give me mine now.

It is no secret that our country has swindled the working class out of our God-given right to laziness. Consider the subject of retirement. Here is a word that implies that we have worked, become tired, rested a little, worked some more and now we are tired again. Thus "re-tired." Correct me if I'm wrong, but hasn't someone snatched half of our retirement? Whatever happened to the first half, the "tired" phase? No doubt some former Surgeon General guided by the advice of a tyrannical father convinced us that laziness was harmful to our health and ordered disclaimers placed on all leisure merchandise that read: WARNING: WHILE HARD WORK HAS NEVER KILLED ANYONE, WE CANNOT SAY THE SAME FOR RELAXATION, SO REST AT YOUR OWN RISK.

The government officials probably figured that if more people skipped the "-tirement" phase of their carrier and continued working through their middle years, the government would collect more tax dollars. And it has worked…to a point. The human body, however, is not so easily duped. The much-heralded mid-life crisis is not some mirage we trip over on our way to death. It is a predictable response to our contemporary work habits. It is our body's way of signaling recess period and advising us to take a few years off. Enjoy an extended vacation, learn a new trade, go back to school or just plain go fishing. It is the first installment of our retirement. A rest area on the road of life, if you will.

Older, more civilized cultures recognize this need for time away from work and reward their citizens with afternoon siestas and long vacations. These countries understand that when a worker slows his pace and takes time to regroup, he improves the quality of his work. They respect this need for reassessment and retooling of a career. Indeed, a society is deemed "civilized" based on the degree of leisure it provides its peasants. It is a mark of maturity.

But not in America. Here, we just grip another cup of coffee and press on with the next project. And for what? So we can buy a larger house for the kids to trash? Buy a fancier car so the insurance premium doubles? Move up a notch in the rat race? Let's face it. Even if you win the race, you're still a rat.

The idea of saving for retirement is folly, as well. Our government and financial leaders implore us to withhold a few dollars of each paycheck and invest it in an IRA, but any business major knows "inflation" and "return on investment" are but two contestants in a three-legged race. Do as the experts suggest and you will be shocked at how little you have when you retire. Ask the loyal bank tellers of America's defunct Savings and Loans what their retirement was worth after bankruptcy. My solution is simple. I'm taking my retirement while there is still one to be had.

If the experts are correct, my talents will be more in demand as the labor force shrinks. I will bring wisdom and maturity to an industry overrun with brashness and inexperience. While my younger associates are racing off for a quick weekend on the water, I will be working late. My employer will no doubt recognize this dedication and reward me with greater responsibilities. And isn't that what we truly desire in our maturing years? A sense of worth? A feeling that our work makes a difference? Who wouldn't like one last chance to carve their initials into the tree of life? Retirement should be a reward, not some ceremonial watch presented to us when we are too blind to "sea" which is why I refuse to go with the tidal flow. I'm going to take advantage of the current over-supply of workers and enjoy my "tired" phase while I still have my health. It makes more sense than slugging it out for some tiny parcel of paradise when I'm too whupped to enjoy it. My family is a bit uneasy with this prospect, but they'll get over it. Bennie used to worry that I wouldn't find a job, but when she realized I was nothing more than a lazy, boat-bum romantic with a knack for doodling in print, she wasn't upset. She was glad I had finally found a vocation.

My calendar is booked solid with interesting islands and exotic ports I hope to visit in the coming years and I have enough writing projects to keep me busy into the next century. I believe the best guarantee for a successful retirement is to invest in yourself. At least then when your worn out portfolio goes belly up you'll know you didn't squander your time and talents.

OYSTERS ROCKEFELLER

The price of oysters just went up. Not that they were any bargain before—what with the ravages of red tide and all. What makes these rich critters especially difficult to swallow is the notion that the increase is directed at boaters alone. How much of an increase, you ask? Try 400%! Now that's an Oyster Rockefeller!

You won't find this increase implemented in restaurant or seafood houses. You won't find the waitress at the Net House asking if you own a boat, then adding an extra $10 to your meal. No, this price subsidy is passed along through more devious methods at a place notorious for high-handed shenanigans—the boat yard. That's right, it all comes down to those tin-based bottom paints we like and their harmful effects on shellfish. It seems the oysters in our marinas got to looking kind of puny, then grotesque and then they just up and died.

Busy-body environmentalists rushed in with their water samples and lab reports and announced that tin-based bottom paints were leaching out and killing the oysters. Well slap me silly and call me stupid, but isn't that what bottom paint is *supposed* to do? I mean, what is a barnacle if not a working-class oyster? It only stands to reason that if a blue-collar barnacle can't hang with a boat hull, a wimpy little oyster doesn't stand a chance either.

This group of concerned do-gooders concluded that recreational boats spent too much time in marinas poisoning stagnant waters and killing wildlife, so they went crying to the state legislators and the next thing you know, local governments had banned bottom paints with the leaching ingredient TBT. They exempted commercial vessels, such as freighters and warships, however, because boats like these move around a lot. (Hey, I'm not making this up. That's really what they said.) What this means for us is that bottom paints will return to the dull rust color of copper-based paints. Gone are the bright greens, blues and reds. Now it's rose and rust. More importantly, it means more haul-outs for scraping and painting, probably once a season for coastal boats. And, of course, that means more money out of your pocket.

As a public service, I did a little figuring just to see how much this environmental stand was going to cost me. At a conservative two hundred dollars a painting, divided by twenty seafood dinners a season, divided by fifteen oysters per dinner, it came to 66 cents per oyster. And I don't even clam in my slip except for an occasional snap shackle or inebriated crewmate.

Now don't get me wrong. I'm not in favor of killing oysters, clams or any other shellfish with chemical pollutants. Lord knows we've dumped enough trash in the waters as it is. But it seems to me the government has acted hastily in this matter. Instead of banning tin-based paints for recreational boats, why not take the approach of the commercial vessels and pass a law requiring us to move our boat and go sailing more? Say, twice a week at a minimum. If someone is found slothful in their duties, fine them a hundred bucks. A second offense, five hundred. If through repeated fines it becomes clear the armchair sailor has no intention of using his boat, confiscate the vessel and give it to some poor soul who has the heart but not the means.

Do this and everyone wins. The oysters live. The bottom paints remain bright and cheap. The absent boat owners are freed from the guilt and responsibility they feel for not using their vessel, while at the same time, some romantic chap with a tattered Sunfish could suddenly find himself the proud owner of a Hinckley. Best of all, we have a valid excuse to call the office and tell them we'll be out for a few days. I can hear it now.

"Sorry, boss. I'll be off Tuesday and Wednesday. Wish I didn't have to, but it's that new law, you know. Twice a week now...No sir, I don't mind looking around while I'm down there. What did you have in mind? A thirty-footer? No problem. I'll see what I can find."

Now, if they would only legislate sex.

RUN AWAY RIDE

I received a disturbing note from my marina today. It said they had found my Ranger 33 wandering the creeks of Oriental unattended. It seems *Walter Mitty* sailed to the entrance of the Whittaker Creek channel before someone had the good sense to haul him back home. My guess is Walter got a case of cabin fever and set out for Ocracoke. This wouldn't be the first time my boat has run away.

I hesitate to mention the incident, because it's a little embarrassing to have your boat running loose in the dead of winter. The next thing I'll hear is that Walter has fallen in with the wrong crowd and vandalized someone's property. It would be just like him to get caught trashing a dock box with a bunch of Bayliners. Of course the owner would probably expect me to pay for the damage even though I didn't do it.

This isn't the first incident of this sort A few years ago I lost a boat in Beaufort. I had set two anchors for the currents in Taylors Creek and stayed aboard long enough to make sure both would hold with the changing tide. I left that Saturday afternoon confident my ComPac 16 would still be waiting for me the next day, but when I returned Sunday morning, she was gone. I jogged anxiously down the boardwalk, hoping I had miscalculated her position in the harbor, but finally I had to admit she'd broken loose and floated away. I hopped in my dinghy and started off for the Beaufort Inlet, hoping to catch my small sailboat before she went to sea. As I was racing through the fleet, a nice lady flagged me down and explained that they had watched my vessel drag anchor earlier that morning. When it became apparent to them no one was aboard, they retrieved it with their dinghy and brought my runaway ride alongside their vessel. I thanked them, of course, but I still suffer from a slight bout of nausea every time I recall that empty hole in the anchorage.

Not long afterwards, I had a similar experience with my Nimble 20. That incident centered on a temporary anchorage at the Camp Don Lee sailing facility. A violent nor'easter elevated the creek level above the canoe dock and during the height of the storm my Nimble drifted over the pier. When the water subsided my Nimble settled on the rotting planks, leaving me hard aground and very uneasy about absentee parenthood. I thought I'd finally outgrown such nonsense when I bought *Walter Mitty*, but then today I got this note telling me he'd run off.

We adopted Walter last spring and I've suspected for some time that he hasn't been happy with his new home. He had it pretty good with his previous owners. They would come down once a summer, spend a weekend aboard and make sure the marina staff was maintaining Walter's appearance. When some piece of hardware looked questionable, they'd buy him a new one. If he messed his bottom, they would have it cleaned immediately. When they sensed he was being neglected, they would purchase him some fancy new gadget to make him feel more like a yacht.

Walter liked all this attention and it showed. He never ran away from his former owners.

Walter Mitty was a spoiled yacht. But all that changed when I stepped aboard. Instead of cleaning his decks and tuning his rig, we went sailing. I didn't even check to see if we had enough fuel in the tank to get us back to the marina—were we inclined to return. Walter didn't care for this tough-love approach and he said so by hacking and coughing and spewing toxic fumes all the way out the channel. I put an end to that nonsense as soon as we reached deep water by raising the sails. Walter has slowly accepted this new diet of discipline and his performance has improved because of it. He doesn't hiss and moan as much, though he still throws things over the side when he's ready to go home. The last time it was a winch handle. So while the news that Walter wanted to go sailing so early in the spring isn't surprising, his doing so without me shows just how far the two of us have drifted apart—in this case, a full creek's worth.

Still, if I'm going to spend $69 on a wayward child, I want an explanation, so I called the marina to see what his problem was.

"While you were in the Bahamas, a cold front moved through and your pennant broke," they explained.

"What's a pennant," I asked.

"That's the rope that runs from your cleat to the mooring. Yours chaffed through and the boat drifted across the creek and got stuck in the mud."

"Any damage?" I asked.

"None that we could see. We towed her back and put a new line on for you. It was no big deal."

Not if it was the first time, maybe, but I'm tired of being haunted by this nightmare. I'm so paranoid that my heartbeat increases every time I turn into the marina and look towards my mooring. Honest to goodness, I peep out across the creek fully expecting to see a hole where my boat used to be. You would think a guy who runs aground as much as I do could get his boat to stay stuck when he wanted to, but I can't. It seems when I want to stop cruising, I can't and when I'm ready to leave, I don't.

I guess the only way to break Walter of his wayward wanderings is take him with me to the Bahamas next year. At least then we'll both be stuck in the same place.

FALLING COCONUTS

I heard a coconut fall this morning.

It landed just as I was easing into the cockpit to enjoy a fresh cup of coffee. Woven into the forlorn howl of the northerly wind was a soft but resounding "thump." The boys were asleep in their bunks, so they didn't hear it. Neither did Bennie. She was up at the bathhouse. I don't think any of them would have paid it much mind anyway. They don't have the ears for it yet.

I had settled onto a dew-laden seat cushion in the corner of the cockpit to let the coffee cool. An energetic cold front from two days earlier had left the sky a few shades darker than what is as generally accepted as Carolina blue and some careless young angel in her haste to be home by sun-up had lost a few feathers from her silken wings. Now they were caught in the sky like wisps of cotton candy stuck on a turquoise blouse. A sudden breeze scattered the vapors of steam from the amber broth, so I sipped, scalding my lips and myself for not being more patient. The gust was a hardy one for such an early hour and coming from the northwest like it did, I expected it to have the flavor of coolness. A wave of heat enveloped the boat instead. It was not the damp, pasty heat of summer, but a clean, brisk warmth like that of the tropical trades. The clear skies, warm winds and dry air unleashed the misplaced excitement I had felt last winter in Marsh Harbor and with that one breeze, all dread and remorse I felt for the coming of winter was swept away.

The coconuts were beginning to fall—and not a moment too soon.

I don't know about you, but this was a tough year for cruising. It started off with that new User Fee tax imposed by Congress and it's been up wind from there. Sailing this summer just wasn't as much fun as I'd remembered in years past. It was more work than play—more time spent at the slip repairing the same problem over and over. There were too many Saturdays spent reaching for a socket set and a screwdriver when I should have been reaching for a nearby anchorage. Too many nights spent slapping mosquitoes and gnats and too many hot and sticky days. There were tainted comments concerning the virtues of sailing and too much money wasted on yard bills, engine repairs and groceries for passages that we never made. It all went wrong at the worst possible time and the cumulative effect is that my dream, my one passion in life, is on a lee shore. Worst of all, I'm beginning to think it's not worth the trouble.

It all came to a boil around Labor Day when the family called a meeting of the crew and slipped me the black spot, as it were. You see, I was supposed to sail to Beaufort from Oriental and meet my family at the Dock House. I had just set the main and jib to take advantage of the breeze and was about to exit Core Creek when the engine stopped, leaving me a few hundred yards short of open water. I tacked my way across Bogue Sound, testing the boundaries of the narrow ICW and was starting to bear off for Town Creek when I bumped and ran aground. A powerboat offered to pull me off, so I secured his line to my bow and pointed him back towards the main channel, indicating the route from which I'd come. Meanwhile, a fisherman who'd also stopped to help, fastened a line on the stern. I couldn't make him understand that I also wanted his line on the bow, so I gave up trying and just pointed back to the channel. I instructed both vessels to pull at once, which they did with great earnest, but in opposite directions. It was just as well, I guess. Neither was headed for the channel. Later that evening, as we were calculating the cost of repairs, towing charges and dockage, my crew announced their intentions.

"We've talked about it amongst ourselves and we've decided we're ready to sell the boat, combine our money with another family and buy a cottage at the beach," my wife Bennie explained. "You can still go sailing. We'll set aside enough cash so you can buy a Sunfish."

"And I'll still go with you sometimes," Win added, "as long as it's not too rough."

My eyes revealed the shock and hurt. "Just give it some thought," Bennie suggested, leaving me to ponder a future with a crew of fair-weather sailors. So I will. In a few days I should be clearing Whale Cay Passage and bearing off for Marsh Harbor on the strength of those warm, southeasterly trades I was telling you about. I will be sailing down to the islands on a friend's boat and will have ample time to consider my crew's offer to abandon ship. While I'm sitting in the lineup at White Sound, surfing those small barrels on Elbow Cay, I will review my family's offer and review their proposal. As I take a break from spear fishing on the backside of Manjack Cay I'll consider their concerns and try to put our situation in perspective. But sell the boat? I wouldn't count on it. My dream may be worn and frayed around the edges, but it's nothing that a Goombay Smash can't cure—provided it's laced with a healthy dose of fresh coconut milk, of course.

CHILL OUT

Why is it I can't ever remember how hot it was in July or how cold it can get in February? It would save me a lot of pain if I could commit this agony to memory.

I recall complaining about the heat of this past summer, but I can't remember the heat itself. I know it was hot, because I remember pedaling my rental bike all over Ocracoke Island in search of two blocks of ice. Heat and a poorly insulated ice box on my boat had produced a run on this essential cruising commodity and the ice truck from Manteo was stranded in Buxton with a busted transmission, a cargo of clear plastic bags filled with cold water and not much else. While I'm no nutrition expert I do know over-ripe bologna when I smell it, so I was trying to salvage our main course by hunting blocks of ice. I didn't find any, bought crushed instead, then set out again the next morning on the same mission with similar results. There may be worse ways to spend one's leisure time on an extended summer cruise, but I can't think of a one.

I remember sitting in the cockpit under a threadbare bimini wondering what the Anchorage Inn charged for one of those rooms overlooking the harbor. I remember promising myself I'd call ahead next year and check into it. At least then I could look out across the anchorage at all those miserable slobs broiling in the sun and be glad it was them and not me but for now I was them so the fantasy only made me feel worse.

Well all is forgiven now because fall is here. The air is clean and cool and perfect for sailing. The winds are steady and seasoned with the fragrance of dried leaves, fresh cut grass and seasoned beef on the grill. It's the kind of weather that makes me slip on a sweater in the morning and sandals in the afternoon. I'm no longer content to throw on a pair of shorts with its matching paint-speckled T-shirt. I want to dress up a bit. I've had to adjust the bindings on my Topsiders to accommodate my rag socks and I'm looking more and more like the cover-stud on a

Land's End catalog. Yesterday, as I was coming down the channel, I caught the sweet exhalation of an oak log blazing in a fireplace. I know it's too early for this sort of thing but I understand that pilgrim's desire to rush the seasons. I do it all the time.

I've always thought it would be nice to be heading south this time of year. A lot of my friends are and you keep rubbing my bow in it. Well I don't care this year. People who sail south for the winter have a schedule to keep. I don't.

This weekend or the one after that, I'll pick my destination based on the movement of the cold fronts and take my time returning Sunday afternoon—or Monday morning. My schedule is open. If the wind's out of the south and I'm ahead of the front, then it's north to Bath, Belhaven or Ocracoke. If the front has already passed and the wind's out of the north, then I'm off to New Bern, Beaufort or Cape Lookout. Every year there is at least one cruise that gets bumped during the hustle and heat of the summer and October is a good month to reschedule that trip. This year it's Wrightsville Beach.

I have friends in Wrightsville Beach and I've always thought it would be nice to set a hook in Banks Channel and wave at the weekend crowd racing back and forth across the bridge. There's usually a good swell running off Masonboro jetty this time of year so the trip will be a sailing-surfing expedition.

Of course, I don't have to go. I can always wait until next spring, but if I do go and return home safely without breaking my board or boat then I'll call the season a success and feel good about my skills as a skipper. I suppose those of you heading south this fall share a similar feeling once you've returned in the spring but you'll have to wait a lot longer than me for that satisfaction. I'll be starting all over again when you're just finishing up but in between then and now is that three-month stretch called winter. Ah, there's the rub.

I can never remember the actual pain of forty-two degrees and twenty-knots of wind but I know it's cold. I remember that much because I recall poking my head out of the companionway last January to test the morning forecast and thinking how relieved I was that my wounded Atomic 4 engine was not up to the journey. Now I fear my enthusiasm for these glorious fall afternoons on the water will entice me to attempt one trip too many, leaving me with a bitter attitude until spring.

This year I hope I've got enough sense to stop sailing while I'm ahead of the wind and use the cold months to plan my spring cruising schedule. I hope I've suffered enough and learned enough to use the shorter days to tinker on my boat and reduce my list of ever expanding boat projects. I hope I'll know better than to chance a weekend on the water in January and ruin a good thing.

But I doubt I will. Experience may be a cruel teacher but for a slow learner like me sometimes this sort of "outside" tutoring is needed to "chill" the enthusiasm of my winter wanderings.

LIFE TO WINDWARD

I was out sailing with an accountant friend recently when he launched into a commentary on the recent tax changes and their effects on boat ownership. Due to the nature of his work, he spends considerable time following the news out of Washington and bemoaning the fiscal abuses of our impotent legislators. So it was with a somber posture that he turned to me and declared, "Well, Jones, thanks to the new tax laws, I guess you'll have to sell the *La Vie Dansante* and give up sailing."

"Since when did taxes have anything to do with sailing?" I asked.

"Let's face it," he continued. "That lackadaisical work ethic of yours is reflected in each paycheck and you can barely afford this boat now with all your other debts. The only way you've managed it this far is by deducting the interest."

"And I'll keep right on managing just fine. Who knows? It might qualify as a second home."

"Not if Senator Danforth and the Finance Committee have their way, it won't. Besides, I don't think a Sterno stove and Porta Pottie is what the IRS had in mind when they ruled a boat needed sleeping, cooking and toilet facilities to qualify as a second residence."

"Well, as his surname would suggest, the good Senator must have his head in the sand if he thinks disallowing boats as a second home is going to compel wealthy yacht owners to pay their fare share of taxes. If a yacht owner is truly 'wealthy' and can afford a $200,000 boat, then he can certainly buy a vacation home of greater value and claim it as his second residence. Any yacht he owned would be nothing more than a large dinghy docked out back of his Palm Beach estate. If Danforth were to research the issue, he'd find most of the people who own boats are just middle-class folks like me who couldn't afford a true second home at the coast even if we wanted one...which we don't! Doing away with the deduction is only going to place another burden on the already heavy-laden. I'll grant you a few poor souls might panic and sell their boat if they lose the deduction, but not me. I'm going to keep right on sailing, with or without the deduction."

"That's not a very wise investment decision."

"Wise investment? When has sailing ever been anything other than a large expense—the proverbial hole in the water?"

"But don't you see? You could take that same money and invest it in stocks and pay cash for your dream boat when you retire."

"You've missed the point, my dear man. I'm already retired."

"No, you're just lazy."

"Same thing."

Overwhelmed by the beer and sheer stupidity of my argument, he soon dropped the subject and his chin to his chest and began to snore.

Reflecting back on that conversation a few days later, I realized that the tax thing was just a symptom of a much larger problem for my friend. He had fallen into the trap of letting outside forces set his priorities and curtail his thirst for life. I know. I've been there myself.

I used to be a bottom-line man too, concerned only with the best value for the money. I was striving for as much of the green cheese as I could devour, hoarding it from all others, repressing the dreams of my family and self. Isn't that the patriotic thing to do? Isn't that what we teach our children—deny yourself for the good of others?

So off I went to the schools of higher learning to get a job, not an education. I took the job because I enjoyed the money, not the career. When I finally had the money, I based my purchases on social acceptability, not real desire. (What difference does it make which type automobile you drive as long as it gets you to the marina safely?) I was well into the rat race before I realized I was living my life by a pattern set before me by others. My parents, my employers, my friends, the advertisers. And I was miserable.

That's when I called in my first mate, re-plotted our course and fell off the wind, you might say. It wasn't that our point of sail was bad. We were just (penny) pinching up too much and beating ourselves to death. I worried that without some course adjustment we would soon reach that mid-life leeward mark like so many others before us and abandon the race—or worse, the crew.

Lord knows there are plenty of those types out there. You find them cruising the waterways in the summer and the islands in the winter. They are the ones who sold their house, cars and furniture, cashed in the life insurance policy and sailed off to see the world. When you meet one they all say the same thing. Do it now and let's face it, the idea of buying a boat and sailing to paradise is a popular tune on the Fantasy Hit Parade. We all sing that little number from time to time. I can't think of anything more romantic than seeing this beautiful planet with all its different landscapes and people from the cockpit of a yacht. But I'd be shamed to death knowing I left my parents and in-laws standing on the dock as they watched their children and grandchildren sail away. There's no guarantee everyone would be in attendance when we returned.

So our approach is to take retirement a little at a time. Stretching weekends into weeks until they become a month. Not sailing away forever—just for a while. If that means moving into a new job that allows for more cruising time, so be it. The freedom and happiness more than offset the loss of income. While all our friends are moving into larger and more prestigious homes, we're looking to buy a few more feet of boat. When those same friends come to us and announce proudly that they've been accepted into the country club, we offer our congratulations and promise to drop them a note from the Bahamas.

You see, I don't want to save my pennies for a "someday" of cruising, which may never come. I want to sail new waters and visit exotic harbors while my health is still an asset, not a liability. I want to cruise with my children while they are still young enough to learn the lessons sailing teaches. I want to see their self-confidence grow as they take the helm in rough weather and learn the lessons of teamwork and obedience, responsibility and trust. I want them to befriend people who are of a different culture and color and realize that it's not the package that is important, but the heart inside. I want to grow closer to my wife through enriching experiences and avoid the decay of boredom which comes when everything is prepackaged and preplanned and goes according to schedule—which sailing never does.

That is why I'm not concerned with the new tax laws or Senator Danforth and his committee, though it seems odd to me that a man from a state five hundred miles from the ocean could claim to be an expert on yacht owners. Elk hunting and buffalo chips, yes. Sailors, no.

But then, taxes and the weather are a lot alike—you can't do much about either and they're always changing. About all you can do is seek (tax) shelter from the rain and continue on course. And never give up the ship. No matter what the cost.

What follows are a few of the comments to the Editor of Coastal Cruising Magazine that prompted Eddie's Hard Aground column; Moments Frozen in Time. Note: the photograph that spurred so much discussion is featured on the back cover of this book...for the last time we hope.

"Eddie Jones is someone I can relate to as I have most of his habits. At last, I found someone like me."

"Are the moronic ramblings of that gross incompetent Eddie Jones necessary? Perhaps he and his readership get enjoyment from the fact that he embarks upon his cruising adventures improperly prepared and obviously without any concern for the safety of his crew and his fellow mariners. His incompetence does not require citing, as he regales in relating it at every opportunity. To encourage such slovenly captaincy angers me, as we have problems enough on the water with literally ignorant people, without populating it with stupid people. I also find no comfort in his picture featuring a prominently displayed alcoholic beverage. While there is no implication that he drinks to excess, or even drinks at all while boating, it implies that boating and drinking are compatible activities, which they are not (nor flying, auto driving, etc.) As they say, you can't please everybody and in this instance that's me."

"I'm guessing Eddie Jones is one heck of a fine skipper. I enjoy reading of his miscapades. If we can't laugh at some of the dumb things we've all accomplished, maybe we take our fun too seriously and it ain't no fun no more."

"I think Eddie Jones looks the picture of contentment with that beer in his hand. So what if someone else thinks he should have had a V-8."

"I have never written to a magazine before, although I subscribe to many...but I am literally compelled to take the time and write this letter to you. I am a relatively new subscriber and basically I like the concept of the magazine but I must tell you...I *hate* the photograph of Eddie Jones that appears with his column each month. I am not saying this humorously or lightly. The photo really disgusts me. His sickening sneer coupled with the beer bottle is truly ugly and lends absolutely no class to your image at all. Believe me, I like a beer too, but there is something about this depiction that makes me *not* look forward to opening an issue. I trust you will take my comment seriously. I feel so strongly about the photo that I probably won't renew my subscription if I am force to see his face each month."

"We should all let Eddie be Eddie. It's his choice what hat to wear, whether to hold a beer or soda, etc. Just don't let him change his writing style."

"I agree that excessive drinking and boating, flying, auto driving, swimming, walking, etc is unacceptable. But the photo of Eddie Jones sitting on the dock, having a beer, smiling with relief, celebrating the fact he made it back to the marina again certainly doesn't imply that he endorses being intoxicated at the helm or as a member of the crew."

"I appreciate your response to the gentleman who was so critical of your publication. If he doesn't like the articles and gets angry at reading about Eddie's misadventures, he shouldn't subscribe. Unfortunately, there are some of us who make dumb mistakes and, in fact, just plain screw up. We sometimes run aground, get caught out in the weather we shouldn't be in and do other "stupid" things. But we also learn from them and sometimes even laugh about them later. I find your magazine to be refreshingly different!

"I enjoyed my first issue and want a year's subscription if only to see whether Eddie Jones is allowed to go on appearing with a bottle of beer in each issue."

"I just spent 15 hours "hard aground" on a sand bar waiting for the river to rise and I thought a lot about the fact that no matter how much experience you have there is still room for a little more. Eddie Jones and I would have had a great time together waiting for the boat to float off that bar."

Moments Frozen in Time

I don't know how you came to own a boat but I drifted in to sailing without a plan or purpose. Any wind is the right wind for the man who does not know where he's headed and when I swerved into my first boat show I was buffeted by conflicting facts and fads. Like some nautical neophyte tripping over dock lines and trailer hitches I was easy prey for the barracudas in blue blazers. They exploited my enthusiasm and ignorance and were helped, I suppose, by my mistaken belief that I could steer a sailboat towards some fixed point across a body of water by means of a wooden tiller and soiled sails. I had no previous experience, mind you, but I was encouraged to hear from my salesman that most people profit from their mistakes. Of course I now know that there is no profit in used mistakes and new ones are heavily discounted. From my position in the cockpit of a fiberglass-scented sloop, however, this concept of all (hands on) deck learning seemed like a small investment to make in the pursuit of my dream.

So I bought a boat.

It was a small thing. It was old and leaked and rested on the fractured frame of a rickety trailer outfitted with two flat tires. I could've bought a newer, nicer, dryer ComPac 16 but I figured I was just going to break the darn thing anyway so why not save money and buy one that was already trashed.

I choose New Bern, NC as my first homeport, partly because of its historic importance but mostly because it had a boat ramp. I have two chilling memories of New Bern. The first involves a controversy that once plagued this column and greatly diminished my standing with the Power Squadron types. I'm speaking of the "Picture."

About a year after *Carolina Cruising Magazine* published its first issue I found Bert Quay asleep in a fold up metal chair at the Raleigh Boat Show in Dorton Arena. That was back when Bert was still Editor and the Raleigh Boat Show still had sailboats. We chatted for a while about the focus and direction of the magazine and he finally agreed to consider a piece I'd written. At the time I thought all boating publications made lots of money and paid their writers exorbitant fees. I was a little disappointed that my bride didn't share my enthusiasm for this new vocation, but I knew she would come around to my way of thinking once the paychecks started adding up. Besides, I'd finally found gainful employment on the strength of my two greatest assets—laziness and ignorance.

I learned later that Bert had little use for my first column, but because someone at the magazine had slipped up and accidentally sold an ad they needed some copy to fill in the rest of the page. I can live a month on a compliment—two months if it's delivered with cash. When Bert ran my second Hard Aground column a few months later my level of conceit reached a height it hadn't known since I was elected hall monitor in the second grade. This sudden rise from obscurity to absurdity soon led to other problems, however.

"We need a picture to go with column," Bert said, later that week. "Have you got something we can run?"

"Sure. I got all sorts of pictures."

"I mean something with you on a boat?"

Well, this seemed odd. For some reason I had never felt compelled to have my picture taken on a boat. "What kind do you want," I asked.

"We need a black and white that reflects something of the nature of your Hard Aground material," he continued, "and we need it now."

The next day happened to be Thanksgiving and since the boat was docked in New Bern, I figured I could enlist my wife's cousin as photographer, provided I could drag him away from the football games. At the time Will was sixteen and knew a little something about photography. By this I mean he knew that large color layouts of naked women looked better than out of focus halftones of fully clad men. I felt fortunate to have his services.

Thanksgiving arrived that year with a blast of cold air from Canada. We abandoned our game of tackle football in the front yard because one of our players developed hypothermia and the other was knocked unconscious when the ball struck him on the side of the head. After lunch Will and I packed our coats, sweaters, gloves and camera and drove over to the boat. I had the good sense to carry along "the hat," not because I thought it was silly, but because I thought it stylish. I've since been informed it is not.

The sun was just high enough to provide maximum light for our photo shoot but Will was having difficulty establishing the proper angle. He motioned for me to slide to my left, which I did, but he still couldn't get all of me in the picture.

"It's because the door jam is still blocking your view," I hollered. "Get out of the truck so we can be done with this."

"You're not the photographer. I am," he said, rolling down the window some more. "Maybe if I lean out like this I can get most of you in the picture and still keep the heater blowing on my feet."

"Well, shoot or shut up but let's do something because I'm about to freeze."

"Wait, you need a prop," Will called back. "Hold this."

He tossed me a glass container from the floorboard of the pickup cab. I scrunched back against the bow pulpit and tried to look relaxed. I imagined I was sitting in Hopetown watching the sun set behind the lighthouse. I imagined I was in Key West listening to Buffett or sailing into Cane Garden Bay after a fast passage from Bermuda. I imagined I was anywhere but in New Bern on a cold November day. It was a moment frozen in time. As for the glass container Will asked me to hold for the picture,

I can only say that I have been advised by the legal department of the magazine not to comment on the brand or its contents.

My second memory of New Bern also had its origins at a boat show. I'd spent too much time reclining in the salon of a new Crealock 34 and was once again overcome by the fragrance of new fiberglass. It was a warm day for February and that got me to dreaming about long tacks on this nice new boat, which was a sure sign I'd been bitten by the new boat bug.

Having recovered from previous bouts with this illness I knew that the only way to fight the infection was to get on my own broken boat and rediscover how miserable and costly sailing can be. Early the next morning my oldest son and I headed over to Duck Creek for a winter day sail. The temperature was in the seventies with a steady wind out of the south and I had a whole stack of stuff on the dock that I was loading onto the boat. My son was four at the time and it was his job to sit on the grass in his life jacket and watch for snakes. There are no snakes in Duck Creek in February, but he didn't know this and so he took his calling seriously.

A gentle wind kept pushing the boat away from the dock and after several leaps from dock to deck, I'd become pretty good at soaring across the chasm with sails and sandwich fixings. Before my final flight, I turned back to Win and told him he would be next. I stood at the edge of the dock, holding the outboard by its handle and jumped aboard.

Well, almost.

It never occurred to me that a fifty-pound outboard would reduce my hang time. I never even reached the toe rail. I was in the water and going down before I could consider the cold consequences of my reckless conduct. When I was almost to the bottom and out of air I thought that maybe I could increase my odds of breathing again by releasing my grip on the motor. When I reached the surface I locked my arms around the dock piling and welcomed the pain of the little barnacles slicing into my hands and feet. When the cuts and cold finally gained an advantage over fatigue, I crawled up the pole and flopped down on the dock.

"Daddy, are you ok," Win asked. "You didn't see a snake, did you?"

"Not that time. Maybe on my next dive."

After an hour of sitting naked in the car with the heater on full, I'd finally warmed enough to put on my wet clothes and go fishing for my motor. I took two boat hooks and rigged my anchor chain between them and then began to drag the bottom like a trawl door on a shrimp boat. I snagged the motor on the second cast. I don't know what brand of outboard you prefer, but I can only say kind words about Nissan because that motor fired on the second pull and hasn't sputtered since.

With all that had already happened I decided we should go sailing anyway and as I recall it turned out to be a delightful afternoon on the water. Still, I wouldn't recommend this sort of bobbing for outboards to my friends. I wouldn't recommend it to my enemies, either. In fact, I wouldn't even wish it on those people who made fun of my silly brown cap, beer bottle and smirking smile.

For that offense, mere drowning would be too light.

Crew Combatability

"*Don't be taken in by appearances. Just because your friend drinks like a fish doesn't mean he'll take to the water like one. I know. I've had my fill of wieners, whiners and wimps.*"

NAVIGATIONAL ILLITERACY

Mac can't read a chart. He can't drive a boat without running aground either. He mistakes green squares for orange triangles and never seems to know if he's coming or red-right returning. I know he feels badly about this but he shouldn't. Mac is one of the thousands of men who suffer from navigational illiteracy. I know because his wife told me.

We had not seen Mac and Sarah since they moved to Thunderbolt, Georgia, some years ago. Visiting my wife's family always gives me pleasure—if not on arrival then upon departure, but this trip was especially exciting because it held the possibility of puttering around the Sea Islands of Georgia on Mac's forty foot Eagle motor trawler. You may think I despise powerboats because of my love for sailing, but that's not true. I like motorboats, especially trawlers; I just can't afford the fuel. The truth is I'll ride in anything that floats and liberates me from the shackles of land and it doesn't have to do either of them all that well.

I learned about Mac's condition soon after we arrived. Navigational illiteracy is a debilitating disease transmitted orally between the sexes. Apparently Mac caught it from his wife's side of the family. He was a pathetic sight sitting there at the helm with one hand on the wheel and the other cupped around a mug of coffee, his eyes fixed on the shag rug of sea grass stretching beyond the high tide delta. Bennie noted how relaxed he looked mistaking his smile and composed posture for contentment. I wasn't fooled. I could tell immediately something was afoul with his disposition. He had all the symptoms.

Navigational illiteracy attacks the nervous system racking the body with acute seizures. Mac's convulsion began with his eye. Sometimes it's a curled lip or furrowed brow, but with Mac it was a twitching eye. This agitated condition was sparked by Sarah's devoted concern for Mac's command of the moment and the twitching accelerated in proportion to Sarah's increased volume.

"Mac, we're awful close to the shore," she said. "Shouldn't we be over to our right a little more?"

"The chart shows there's plenty of water. See, we're in ten feet."

"Well, it looks like we're out of the channel, to me."

"I think we're fine."

"I thought we were supposed to keep the reds to our left," Sarah continued.

"That's right, dear. That's why I'm over here. The waterway guide says I'm to favor the red side of the channel."

"Well, I think you're favoring it too much."

At this point the conversation came grinding to a halt—as did the trawler. Mac began to fidget with the shift and throttle lever, hoping to drown out Sarah's shrill commands with the booming thunder of the diesel's RPMs as he tried to free the boat from the shoal. Now there's a right and wrong way to do everything and once the mind becomes utterly confused, the wrong way always seems the most plausible. It's a side effect of navigational illiteracy.

"He does this every time," Sarah quietly announced. "It's no wonder I don't enjoy boating."

Mac twisted in his seat and muffled a growl, but was still too preoccupied with the destruction of his transmission to offer a more biting response. "It's called boating experience, Hon. Everybody has to pay their dues."

"'Experience' is what you call all your mistakes." Sarah answered, no longer masking her disgust. Mac lowered his head further and rubbed his twitching eye while working the throttle with his free hand. The fact that Mac ran aground isn't surprising. A lot of us do it with great skill. What marked Mac as a navigational illiterate was Sarah's running commentary of his miserable piloting skills. While many of us long for at least one disciple in our crew, in most cases it's Judas who keeps the ship's log. I know because Bennie came rushing to Mac's defense to declare with great importance that I too suffered from navigational illiteracy.

"Oh don't feel badly about this. Eddie gets stuck all the time," Bennie said. "He can't go anywhere without running aground. Of course part of the reason is that our depth sounder doesn't work and he won't take the time to get it fixed. But if he would just look at the chart sometimes it would help. To be honest with you I don't think he can read the chart. He would never admit that, of course."

Well Bennie's right. I won't admit it. I don't have to. She does it for me.

This petty bantering between Mac and Sarah reveals a disturbing trend in modern navigation. Women are taking a more active role in cruising and they're finding we men are not very good at it. This can be a dangerous thing for women, since it's always risky to be right in matters on which the established authorities are wrong. The boating industry has discovered who the real decision makers are in the buying process and they are beginning to tailor their products to women because they know what we men have suspected for some time. Women like boats and enjoy cruising—they just don't like cruising with us. Men have never been very refined when it comes to sailing's social skills. We stock the icebox full of beer and bait and then act surprised when there's nothing planned for dinner. We scrub the deck, but not the head, yell too much, explain too little and discourage our eager crew with harsh words. It is our mark of insecurity.

No wonder women critique our sailing abilities and ridicule our shortcomings. If the trend in women's pay and career advancement is any indication, however, women will have to be twice as good at piloting, docking and anchoring to be considered half as good as men. Fortunately, this won't be too hard.

At least for my sake, I hope not. I'm ready for Bennie to take the helm so I can fix this depth sounder of mine.

HERE'S SAILING WITH YOU, KID

When you live in a state that's spawned the likes of Jesse Helms, Tammy Faye Baker and Barney Fife, you had best be prepared to receive your fair share of tainted comments from those foreign to Carolina inbreeding. Foreigners visiting from Virginia and beyond often miss the fact that buried beneath the chew-and-spit image of North Carolina's NASCAR landscape with its tobacco fields and pig farms is a state that has produced two Nobel Peace Prize winners in medicine and is home to a number of high-tech companies. The simple truth remains that a great many people still regard North Carolina natives as narrow-minded and dumb.

Thus I wasn't too surprised to find myself reproached by a young lady at last year's Annapolis Boat Show. I had shouldered my way through the horde of worshipers eyeing the Bristol 51.5 and escaped into the relative solitude and warmth of the refreshment tent at Pusser's. I shouted my drink order above the buffet of Buffett tunes blaring from the sub-woofers and was about to dip a shrimp in the hot sauce when the young women confronted me.

"I gathered from your accent that you're from the South," she said.

"Yes'm," said I, wiping the sauce from my chin with the back of my hand. "North Carolina, to be exact."

"Then maybe you can tell me why most Southerners are for George Bush and against women?"

"Didn't know we were," I said with sincerity.

"Well, you are. Polls show the South strongly behind Bush and he's against abortion, so women can expect a tough go of it if he is elected."

I apologized for my lack of knowledge on the issues surrounding the election and Southern stupidity in general. I explained that my method of choosing a presidential candidate relied more on hitting and pitching than moral or economic views. If the American League wins the World Series, I vote Democrat. If the National League wins, I vote Republican. And if, by God's grace, the Atlanta Braves ever win, I'll vote Libation for the Old South. I explained all this and still she persisted.

"Then forget about both candidates for a moment and just tell me this. Is abortion murder and a crime, or is it a right granted by the constitution?"

"I guess that would depend on when life begins," I answered, hoping to escape with my shrimp and beer.

"And when do you think it begins?" she asked, her eyes narrowing.

"As a land cuffed sailor, I can tell you it doesn't begin at the moment of conception, nor does it begin at birth. Life begins when the kids leave home, the dog dies, the minivan is sold and the VCR is exchanged for a reliable radar. Now, if you'll excuse me, I have to excuse myself."

"You mean you're afraid to discuss the issue any further," she asked.

"No. I mean I really have to excuse myself," I said, hurrying off to the men's room.

Of course, I was not completely honest with the lady. Sometimes the house must be sold, too.

The point is, most couples that cruise do so without the assistance of children. They have completed God's commandment to bear fruit and multiply and now these couples enjoy the freedom to do as they please, sail where they please and please no one if they please.

"Youth is such a wonderful and precious time," one mother observed, "I'll be danged if I'm going to waste it on my kids They're grown and gone. Let 'em fend for themselves."

I contend any couple that can successfully merge the unpredictability of sailing and the instability of children and do so without losing either the boat or child, deserves a highway litter sign named after them. Occasionally, someone will suggest that children actually help with the duties of sailing and thus make cruising easier, but this is just too much beer talking. That weathered notion might have had merit a hundred years ago on a farm, but it doesn't work on a sailboat and certainly not on *my* sailboat. Let me give you an example.

Last summer our family took a weekend jaunt from Oriental, NC, to Beaufort, NC. Normally, I am blessed with a willing first mate and a good-natured boy. Together, the three of us have experienced some golden moments on the water. We work hard to make sure everyone has fun and the simple pleasures of nature take precedence over reaching specific destinations.

While crossing Bogue Sound that Sunday morning, our dinghy escaped and fled for a beckoning oyster bed. I began maneuvering alongside so my wife could bring the small inflatable aboard, when suddenly my son's scream pierced the air. He grabbed his hand and began dancing a jig in the main salon. In the confusion of the moment, I missed my wife's instructions, ran over the dinghy and lost a good baseball cap over the side of the boat. While Bennie yelled for me to circle once more, my son continued stomping around on the teak and holly floor with a small battery cable clamped on his finger. I studied the situation, abandoned the tiller and lurched below to free Win's forefinger, then ran back to the helm and barely missed running over the dinghy a second time. The look on my son's face as he stood whimpering in the salon seared my heart. What kind of father would not comfort a child in pain? Only a cruising parent could be so cold.

Some parents realize too late that kids and cruising aren't a perfect match. I found one distraught father at the sailboat show who confessed in private that he was at his wits end.

"I've taken my boys everywhere but they still manage to find their way back home," he said with a healthy dose of sarcasm. I know he was kidding, but sometimes it's true—you just can't get shed of the little critters no matter how hard you try.

"When I was growing up," his wife continued, "teenagers rebelled against their parents, became enchanted with the world and ran off to find themselves. But not our boys. They refuse to leave home. So last month Fred and I ran away instead. We're hoping to set an example for others. When our two boys come home from college, all they're going to find is a 'Dear Boys' letter taped to the refrigerator with last month's mortgage statement."

Some might think that I'm against cruising with kids, but I'm not. I named my boat *The Captain and the Kid* because I wanted to share my love of sailing with my son. Admittedly, cruising with children requires a great deal of patience and effort. Bennie and I miss a lot of late-night gatherings on other boats because Win is exhausted from the day's activities. Often, I sit in the cockpit listening to the laughter from the neighboring craft and wish I could join the gaiety. I know a few couples that are quite sincere when they say their boat is their child. I respect their decision and more than once I have secretly coveted their status. After all, an unruly boat can be sold. A child can only be abandoned with grandparents for the weekend.

But on those days when I see my son grasping the tiller and studying the cat paws on the water, I know I have made the right choice. Children are our hope for the future, our legacy of immortality. What better gift can we offer them than our own dreams?

So here's sailing with you, kid.

DEFROSTING A FRIGID WIFE

Most yacht brokers will tell you that the toughest objection they face from prospective clients has nothing to do with income, hull design, desire, or price. Forget standard features, dealer warranty and resale value. Not even the full-bodied lines of a seductive model splashed across the pages of a brochure can overcome this barrier. Like a dark summer squall looming on the horizon, this ominous presence hovers over the negotiating parties. We husbands know it simply as The Wife.

Yacht brokers are not idiots, despite their apparent distaste for stable and lucrative incomes. They might prefer a forty-hour workweek and the benefits of a pension with hospitalization, but selling boats is their love and passion and thus their misfortune. Each has an explanation for how they fell into this career cul-de-sac and many a story would move you to tears, but it's their job, so they have at it with hope and desperation, sometimes courting hesitant customers for months on end. As one salesman put it; "It's like kissing frogs to find a prince. Some customers are just frogs who enjoy the kissing, so they keep coming back asking to look at more boats. They'll torment you to no end if you let them. The secret is to find the prince quickly."

He suggested the shortest path to a sale often leads around the aroused prospect and straight to the one in charge—The Wife.

"A lot of sales are lost because the salesman failed to include the wife in the negotiations and I confess from experience, that kind of thinking is just plain stupid. When I first got into this business, I had a man stop me at the Annapolis show and ask to look at a 30-footer we were brokering. I showed him the pictures, gave him the spec sheet and figured that like most show stoppers, I'd never see him again. Next day he was back at the show, asking a few more questions, looking at the picture again and I began to think that maybe this guy was for real. The third day when I come back from lunch, I found him standing outside our booth in the pouring rain, wearing his slicker and smiling like a kid who'd cut Sunday school. Suddenly, I began to have visions of a fat commission check. I found a day on the calendar for the sea trial, called a boat surveyor friend who owed me a favor and had the client contact a few banks to arrange the loan. There was no question in my mind but that this guy was SOLD. I was about to ask for his deposit, when he muttered; 'First I have to check with my wife.'"

"Fine," I replied. "Bring her back this afternoon and you can drop off the deposit check then."

"Boy, was that a mistake. I should have never let him get away without that deposit. A few hours later, he comes strolling back down the pier like a 10-year-old kid showing off his pet bug collection. He's pointing at the boats and waving his hands and the whole time The Wife is burning a hole through my blue blazer. When he reached our booth and showed her the picture of the boat up on the board, he asked; "What do you think, dear?"

"Wham! She shoves the spec sheet in my gut and declares that my mother was an unwed woman when I was conceived. She then turns and informs her husband that he will not buy this or any other boat until the mortgage is paid, the kids educated and she has been to Europe. Then, maybe if he is real nice, she might allow him a small Sunfish. She turned and stormed off. Right then and there, I learned who bought the boats in this business."

Other brokers shared similar stories, though none wanted to be identified for fear of retaliation. They admitted, however, that by and large wives are the biggest obstacles they face to closing a deal. But don't go blaming the women. If we men haven't done our homework and prepared our mates for that big moment, then there isn't much a salesman can do to save the day. Building towards the dream begins at home and even then, there is no guarantee she'll warm up to the idea. I know one broker who lost a sale because the man's wife didn't like the other women in the marina.

"I had sold this guy his first boat several years earlier and though he had added a couple of kids, he was still plugging along in that same 19-footer. When he came to see me about moving up, he was cranky and sore and all bent out of shape from sleeping in a cramped V-berth. I found him a good used model in the same line of boats at a very good price. The monthly payments would go up some, but at least his family could cruise without sitting on top of each other. Everything was fine, until his wife got involved."

"She complained that the other wives in their marina were temperamental and conniving, always talking about them behind her back. The younger women in the neighboring slips didn't respect the protocol of others and often paraded around the docks in G-string bikinis. She complained that the ones who did cover up were of the braless variety. I tried reasoning with her, even suggested they move to another marina. But after a while I could tell it was hopeless. I mean, what do you say to someone like that? I leaned back in my chair and told them to go home and reach a compromise. They did. They got out of sailing and joined a bowling league."

If it's bad for the man trying to buy a boat, it's worse for the skipper who owns one and finds out too late in life that his wife hates sailing. It happens more often than we want to admit. I know a guy in Charlotte who bought 51-foot Morgan Out Island sailboat and had it outfitted for world cruising. Sonny had worked and saved and planned for that big day and now, by God, he was going to cruise the islands. He announced his decision, stowed his woman and gear aboard and sailed off for the Island of Bliss. At Point-A-Pitre, in Guadeloupe, his first mate mutinied and gave him the ultimatum: "It's me or the boat."

He made his choice, traded the wife away for a future draft pick and shipped his yacht home to Lake Norman because he discovered that there are only so many sunsets a man can endure by himself. Now Sonny's just a big fish in a little pond.

Women are like that. You can't just warm them up like some microwave dinner. They have to defrost slowly. Women enjoy the attention and coaxing and a good many get nervous when they can't see the next channel marker. To expect a wife with limited boating experience to hop aboard and sail away in search of some vague dream is playing a game of Rushing Roulette. That approach may work for some, but more often than not, she'll go off in your face. A smart husband will score more points and reach his dream sooner if he packs a picnic lunch, loads up the Sunfish and sails across the cove to a sandy beach. Then her memories of sailing will be ones of romance and fun, not fright.

It has taken me years of reading and planning to sketch in the details of my dream. Why should it take my wife any less? While I sit ready to trade my mortgage and minivan for the pristine coves of the Abacos, Bennie is looking at wallpaper with an interior designer. She's redecorating our house and adding a room. Obviously, we do not share the same immediate goals, so mine must wait. Do I mind? You bet, but I know enough to keep my mouth shut and more importantly, I know her companionship is worth the wait.

Good women are like that. They age like fine wine, becoming mellow with time and, in Bennie's case, developing a smoother, more full-bodied flavor. When my days in the Abacos arrive I'll enjoy my love of the islands with the love of my youth, because when it comes to paradise found, that's the only way to arrive.

WOMEN AND LOVE AND BOATS WITH SHERE HYPE

I'm fond of clever sayings. Here's one of my favorites by Mark Twain.

"There is no character, how-so-ever good and fine, but it can be destroyed by ridicule, however poor and witless. Observe the ass: his character is about perfect. He is the choicest spirit among all the humbler animals, yet see what ridicule has brought him to. Instead of feeling complimented when we are called an ass, we are left in doubt."
—*Pudd'nhead Wilson's Calendar*

These days I'm feeling a little like the ass thanks to Shere Hite's new book, *Women and Love*. I had no idea we men were such jerks. I tend to agree with Dennis Conner and feel that the term is better suited to New Zealand's Michael Fay, but Ms. Hite has shown me the error of my ways and some proof that a lot of you women out there feel the same. My wife included. In which case, I apologize to all those women out there that I've ticked off.

It appears, however, as if Ms. Hite failed to include women of the sailing community in her report. At least, she didn't identify her respondents as boaters. Age, education, income, employment, race—all these factors were included in her study. But does her book reflect the attitude of helmswomen as well? Are women sailors also frustrated with their marriages? Disgusted with their husbands? Swapping tales of a different sort in the next slip? Is the male boating fraternity really a cross between Archie Bunker and Popeye? I wanted to find out, so I spent a few days around the docks asking women how they felt about women and love and boats. Their answers reflect the marital bliss of ladies who define themselves as live-aboards, weekend sailors, cruisers and hard-nosed racers. Just to be fair, I also talked with a few trawler types.

Most were happy with their relationships. In fact, a few even suggested boating could toughen a marriage by bringing couples together in ways they hadn't imagined. As one woman put it, "You want to know if my husband is still affectionate after thirty years of marriage? When you spend seven days cruising on a 27-foot sailboat you become affectionate, whether you mean to or not. There's just a certain amount of bumping and nudging that's going to take place. I don't care if he initiates the contact or if it's accidental. As long as it leads to the vee berth, that's good enough for me."

Most of the women to whom I spoke were eager to share their feelings and opinions of marriage, so I've included a few of their comments. Bobbie Stuart sails with her male friend on his Ranger 23. She, too, feels sailing brings couples together. "It's one of those rare activities where I have his complete attention. It's just me and him and the boat out there enjoying nature. There's nothing like seeing your man gaze intently into your eyes and know he hangs on your every word. Words like 'Get your own damn beer! I'll steer the boat.'"

Gretchen Neal sails a 28-foot sloop with George, her husband of eleven years. She describes herself as an average mother and wife and a top-notch first mate. When asked if in her eleven years of marriage she had ever been physically abused she replied: "Dozens of times. There are days I look so bad I'm afraid to go to the office because of what people might say. And the pain. Sometime it's more than I can bear. But despite the booming headaches from the unprovoked jibes and the public humiliation from faulty depth meters, I still love that little boat."

"I meant had you ever been beaten by George?"

"Are you kidding? If he treated me like that I'd have a social worker on his butt so fast he'd think he was wearing Milk bone boxers in a pit bull pen."

Francis O'Brien lives with her husband on a 54-foot motor trawler. They spend the winter cruising down the waterway, running from the cold but we both caught up with them at Wrightsville Beach. I asked Francis how their marriage differed from that of a landlocked couple.

"Well, people who live in houses are usually a little funny about things. I mean, those people could live on boats too, but they want a dry roof over their head, fresh food in the cupboards and the morning paper in their driveway. To them life is logical. Unfortunately marriage is not. It is an illogical proposition conceived in lust. Any good soap opera will prove me out. So when the couple finally gets around to asking, 'Why'd we get married in the first place?'—and every couple does—they're lost. They don't have the foggiest idea how they got there. About all they can do is shake their heads and walk away from the courthouse baffled."

"But not Frank and I. We're not logical. If we were we wouldn't live on a boat. In fact, we spend so much time trying to figure out why we ever bought a boat that we seldom have time to focus on each other's faults. Just when I get fed up and think Frank is about the most worthless creature God created, a pump goes out or a leak springs up and wham, we're at it again together on our hands and knees. Cursing and laughing. Crying and comforting each other. Forgetting that just moments earlier

I was ready to slap him silly. So I guess living on a boat makes for a better marriage. That and being hard of hearing."

Susan Shaffer is a weekend racer and something of a perfectionist. I asked her which was more disappointing, marriage or a poor-sailing boat?

"Without a doubt, sailing a poorly designed boat is worse. People expect husbands to be lazy, inconsiderate, forgetful and oversexed. That's about the only flavor they come in. But buying a shoddy boat? Now there's something to be ashamed of. There's nothing worse than realizing the dream of your life can't beat to windward. It's heartbreaking. About all you can do is dump it on some poor soul who doesn't know any better."

Trixie Davis and her family enjoy weekends on the lake. Like any young, upwardly mobile professional family, they research each purchase thoroughly before reaching a buying decision. Still, they bought a boat. "I guess we got caught up in the dream. We would read about a young couple in *Money* magazine or see an ad for some boating resort in *Southern Living* and think, 'We just have to get one.' So we did. Now our whole family loves boating. There's nothing we'd rather do. But...oh, this is so hard to say...yes, it's true: We owe more on the boat now than it's worth. I know that sounds hard to believe. We've done so well with our other investments. It's really tarnished our financial portfolio."

I asked Betty Thompson which was more dependable, her husband or their cabin cruiser. "In spite of what Ms. Hite says, Fred is more dependable. Not that he's very romantic. His idea of foreplay is rolling over in bed, punching me on the arm and asking if I'm awake. But at least he doesn't cost me money. Not like this boat. On the whole, I'd say Fred is easier to love. At least I can get his engine to start."

So there you are, ladies. An unscientific survey of women and love and boats. If any of you feel this survey flawed and wish to chide my methods, I encourage you to write to our Editor. He's single, handsome and poor but one heck of a skipper. As for me, don't waste your time telling me what a dim-witted ass I am. I'd probably think it was a compliment anyway.

SEA TRIAL

This year it would be different. This year the jury would rule in my favor. Once again I would plead my case before the honorable B.C. Jones, knowing full well she would seek a swift and speedy trial. After all, she was known as one of them "hang 'em high" types and last year's verdict was still fresh in my mind.

"No! Absolutely not! This court rules against the plaintiff and refuses to grant him the necessary funds for a new sailboat. Furthermore, I find the defendant in contempt for even bringing such a silly matter before this bench and order him to perform 30 hours of community service around the house. Now get out of my kitchen before I really get mad. Case dismissed."

But like I said, this year it would be different. This year I would research my case, compile the evidence and produce the necessary witnesses. This would be an appeal even Perry Mason would be proud to try. I began with the basic assumption that my wife was not in favor of my owning a sailboat, large or small. I reached that conclusion during our second year of marriage. Inspired by the sheer beauty of the U.S. Virgin Islands, we'd decided to charter a ketch over to St. Johns Island and wave at the wealthy guests lounging on the sands at the Rockefeller Resort. Ten minutes out of the cove and into Pillsbury Sound, my wife suddenly turned white, then green, then around and over the side. It was a position she would maintain the rest of the day.

I tried explaining that it wasn't the motion making her sick but the half a gallon of Cabernet Sauvignon she had consumed the night before, but she didn't buy it. She just glanced up between heaves and coldly said, "Get me off this damn boat and don't ever mention boat to me again." And with that she was back over the side throwing her breakfast and my dreams to the fish.

So I learned to do without the luxuries others enjoy. A queen-size bed in the aft stateroom, ample locker space, functional galley, standing headroom, wet bar, navigation table. But no more. This year, with or without her consent, I would better my sailing comfort. I would purchase a vessel designed for blue-water cruising and give up my hand-worn tiller for one of those stylish silver wheels standard with pedestal steering. As a preliminary move, I asked if she would accompany me to this year's boat show. What could it hurt? Maybe she'd find something she liked and we could reach an out-of-court settlement.

"I'll go to the Home and Garden show, the Christmas show, that big redneck car show. I'll even go with you to that dumb gun and knife show, but I'm not going to a boat show this year or any other year and that settles that."

Some settlement.

Determined to see this thing through to *The People's Court* if necessary, I grabbed my wallet and camera and went searching for the boat of my dreams. I was surprised at the outpouring of advice and help I received. Whoever says money can't buy happiness has never perused a boat show. At the first booth, a tanned fellow in his mid thirties greeted me with a firm handshake and asked what qualities I was looking for in my next yacht. How many feet, shoal draft or winged keel, where did I do most of my sailing, did I enjoy racing or cruising or both? When I finally worked around to sheepishly asking "How much?" for such a fine vessel, he replied with astonishment, "Oh, I'm not the salesman. He's the one down there by the table. I just happen to own a similar model, except mine's three years older. But I'll tell you what. There's not a finer sailboat on the market."

I was about to go down and speak with the salesman when I realized I'd found my key witness. Who better to sell my case before Judge Jones than a happy owner? Forget the salesman. She'd have him for lunch if it came down to a confrontation, anyway. No, this fellow would do just fine. I walked back and began with the questions. Was he married? Have any children? Did his wife sail? How did he get her involved? Had sailing made their marriage stronger? Lovemaking better?

"My wife loves sailing," he responded. "In fact, I was content with the Catalina 22 we owned two boats ago. She's the one who keeps insisting we move up." Here was a man to be envied.

"There was a time when I couldn't even get her on a blow-up raft," he continued. "Oh, she liked the beach okay, but she didn't trust the water at all. I was getting desperate. So one day on a whim, I bought two tickets on one of those Bahamas cruise ships. No way could she pass that up. And you know what, it worked. We took long evening strolls along the promenade deck, rang the bell on the charge cards when we pulled into Nassau, sipped rum punch around the pool at the Merv Griffin's casino and swam naked in the waters off Paradise Island. I gotta tell ya, that was one heartbroken woman when we walked down the gang plank and headed home."

"But of course you didn't buy her a luxury liner," I protested.

"I didn't have to. Neither one of us was up to all that cleaning and scrubbing. Those babies are BIG. Instead, I told her we should buy a small sailboat until we could afford something larger. She agreed, on the condition that we make serious plans to cruise the Bahamas. That was five seasons ago, just before we bought that Catalina I was telling you about. Last winter we spent three gorgeous weeks cruising the Exuma Cays. And to think it all started with that cruise ship."

I was stunned. I'd been going about this thing all wrong. I thanked the man, marched right out of the show, drove to the nearest travel agent and booked an outside-upper-deck room. Then I went home and told Judge Jones I loved her and presented her with the tickets. (Just the words, "I love you" nearly sent her into shock.)

Did it work? Almost. I still don't have the boat of my dreams, but the urge isn't as strong these days. Instead, I have one top-notch first mate who can spot the shoals on a cloudy day and prepare a mean Bloody Mary on a windward tack. And in my book, that's better than any old pedestal steering system.

MAIDEN *HELL* VOYAGE

Bennie recently commented to our friend Betty Cone that we were moving up to a larger sailboat so our family could cruise without sitting on top of each other. Betty laughed. She laughed loud and she laughed for a long time and then she took Bennie aside for some counseling.

Betty Cone is not a sailing widow, but she could have been. She and her husband Caesar have owned a place at Lake Norman so long they can remember when living at "the lake" meant you had a permanent campsite at the Lake Norman Yacht Club. The Cones don't own a large sailboat. Instead, they have just about every type of watercraft imaginable. Two sailboards, a paddleboat, a Hobie Cat, a fleet of jet skis, a Stiletto catamaran and a radio-controlled sailboat. You get the impression there's an itch just out of reach that is trying to get scratched. Caesar's talents as a sailor make him a valuable asset on any vessel and he has a lot of friends with big boats who request his assistance when moving their yacht here to yonder. Caesar can go sailing whenever he likes and does so quite often. So how come the Cones don't have a big boat of their own? Just ask Betty.

"If you want to know what it's like to take your family sailing, pick a weekend when you've got plenty of things you'd rather be doing, gather the family together *on* the kitchen table with a cooler of soft drinks and cold cuts and spend the weekend on the table tearing ten-dollar bills into tiny pieces. That's what cruising is like!"

At least, that's what she told my wife as our family prepared our new-old Ranger 33 for its maiden voyage. Before we took borrowship of this Ranger we had owned a red Snark, a ComPac 16 and a Nimble 20, moving up in degrees and feet as our family increased in numbers. When we sailed on the Nimble with just one child, we could plan our passages around Win's nap so that time on the boat was limited. In the morning Win and I would eat breakfast aboard, then ride bikes into Oriental, play on the swing set or go exploring in the dinghy while mom stowed the gear and provisions and enjoyed some single time. The morning activities helped pass the time and drain Win's energy level. We would try to leave the dock around eleven and during that first hour Win was usually engrossed in the sailing activities. Lunch held his attention for another 30 minutes and by 1:00 pm; he was ready for his nap. Fatigue and the motion of the boat kept him down for about two hours. After the nap came a small snack and then it was time to be wherever we were going. Others might have a different process for planning a passage, but all our coastal cruising was framed around this five-hour window.

These successful voyages led me to believe that what worked with one child would work with two. In fact, I was naive enough to think that the two boys might actually entertain each other and thus extend our sailing time. That was before I caught Win throwing diapers over the side of the boat and focusing his gaze on his infant brother.

"Hey, you're not throwing trash in the water," I asked Win the way we parents ask a thing to which we already know the answer. "How do you think God feels about what you've just done?" I asked.

"He'll forgive me," Win remarked. "That's his job."

Right then I knew I had a cutthroat crew that couldn't be trusted on the high seas or Low Country coastlands. On this particular passage we were heading to Cape Lookout. We had spent several weekends preparing the boat and family for the cruise. Mason, our youngest, had never been away from the dock for more than two hours, so he and his mother were both a bit uneasy about the voyage. Win was just ready to be any-where other than at the dock and I was anxious to see what was going to break, because something always breaks on my boat. By the time we finally reach the Cape, the Neuse Sailing Association crowd had already gathered together in a friendly raft-up, so to keep from disturbing their good time, we anchored some distance away. The trouble began later that evening when Bennie began to prepare dinner.

"The stove doesn't work," she said the way a wife announces a fact that clearly implies you are to blame. "Did you pump it up before we left?"

"Yea, I pumped it up before we left."

"Did you add alcohol?"

"No, I thought it had alcohol."

"Well, it doesn't. Put some in."

I did, but of course now there was no way to pressurize the tank since the pump was in the dock box back at the marina.

"How about if you fire up the propane grill and heat some water on that?" Bennie suggested.

"That's a good idea, but all three of those little green propane bottles are empty."

"All right," she said shoving a cold hot dog in my face. "Here's supper."

We opted for bologna and cheese sandwiches for dinner and the crew went to bed cranky. The next day we discovered the shower pan didn't drain. To prevent the soapy water from spilling over into the cabin sole, we scooped it up with a plastic cup and poured it into the toilet. The boys didn't seem to mind this inconvenience, but Bennie had to be reminded on several occasions that this activity could be fun.

"So far, cruising on this bigger boat isn't much better than cruising in our small Nimble 20," she hollered from behind the bathroom door. "And it's more expensive."

To ease the growing hostility on board, the boys and I dinghied over to the lighthouse to explore the East beach. On our way back across the Bight, the tiny Mercury 2.2 outboard died. You know me well enough by now to guess that I had neglected to stow the oars onboard our inflatable, so there I was with two small children in the noonday heat, drifting out into the Atlantic on a falling tide with a wife who was half hoping that we wouldn't return at all.

You see, while we were gone, Bennie had discovered that we were out of water and ice. By the time I got the outboard running again, Mason had cried himself to sleep and collapsed in a puddle on the floor of the Avon, which was a blessing since his older brother was still looking for an excuse and opportunity to toss him overboard. Heading home Monday morning, the exhaust manifold rusted off and began discharging toxic fumes into the cabin. I opened the cockpit locker so we could air out the cabin but the noise and heat proved too much, so we closed it and told everyone to stay on deck. While the rest of the NSA crowd scurried home on their nice new boats, we limped along under sail and smoke at a paltry three knots.

I admit I've made mistakes, but I have never made the mistake of claiming that I never made mistakes, so now when our family goes sailing, we don't take showers onboard unless it's with a sun shower bag. We use a Coleman camping stove instead of the fancy one that came with the boat and I'm currently in the market for a good used outboard. I'd love to have a newer, nicer boat, like my buddies over there in the NSA, but my lackadaisical work ethic continues to hamper this lavish lifestyle I desire. I've noticed over the years that everyone gets about the same number of breaks in life, but it's the timing that makes the difference. Take ice, for example. The rich get it in the summer and the poor in the winter.

In my case, I have an old boat with a new family when what I really need is a new boat and an old family. Of course by the time my "ship" comes in, my old family will be too busy with their own wives and kids to go sailing with me on my new boat, so I guess I ought to give thanks and enjoy the blessings I have.

And I do.

CRUISING WITH WIENERS, WHINERS AND WIMPS

You never know how many friends you have until you buy a yacht and then, like mosquitoes at dusk, they're all over you. Friends, relatives, old acquaintances, old lovers. They strike with brutality, each needling you for an invitation.

It's not that these dockside moochers are rude, mind you—just misinformed. To them, nothing could be more relaxing than a jaunt down the waterway to some historic coastal village, nothing more romantic than a moonlit anchorage in a secluded cove, nothing more invigorating than salt spray stinging their face as the leeward rail digs in. Of course, nothing could be further from the truth.

I know. I've had my fill of wieners, whiners and wimps.

I've become leery of conversations that begin with "Gee, Ed, when ya gonna take me sailing on your boat?"

So I've adopted a patented response. I lie.

"I'd really love to," I begin, "but the wife's cleaning the teak right now and though she does good work, she is messy. Then there is this guy I hired to do some cabinetry work in the main salon. His approach is to start out slow, then taper off. I could've had another boat built in less time. So you see, now is not a good time. But we'll go soon. I promise."

A great many boaters are closet yachtsmen like me. We own, but don't want to let on that we own, if you know what I mean. We have witnessed what notoriety has done to others and we fear for our sanity. We have watched boat owners pursued by relentless friends until at last the poor soul surrenders and agrees to take the man and his family cruising. Two days later our friend is back in his slip, angry and sullen, vowing never to speak to the man again. It needn't be this way. Not if you subscribe to the axiom that a friend in need is a friend to flee.

As a whole, we closet yachtsmen are a sneaky bunch. We hide boating periodicals when guests arrive and lie about our weekend activities, purporting to visit distant relatives. If by chance someone uncovers our malady, we recount the weak moment that led to the purchase of our vessel and assure them that the craft is now for sale. All moral implications from such a little white lie pale in comparison to a weekend of whining, squeamish, tedious guests. Don't be taken in by appearances. Just because your friend drinks like a fish doesn't mean he'll take to the water like one.

Still, one will occasionally slip past even the best defenses, as happened with my friend John. (That's not Pendo's real name, of course. He wanted me to protect his identity.) Some time ago I promised John I'd take him sailing and this summer we finally put it together. On the way over to the boat he happened to mention that he was a whiner.

"A what?" I asked.

"A whiner. A malcontent. I complain a lot."

He said I took too long preparing the boat and was disappointed we couldn't leave for Beaufort that evening. He grumbled that there wasn't much action in Oriental and seemed especially distraught that an evening of barhopping required only 40 minutes. He was awake at six the next morning, complaining that there were too many bugs in his hair to sleep. He wondered why we couldn't go any faster under power. The trip to Beaufort took too long and the sandbar party was too small. The bars closed too early. He said it was too hot to sleep and asked if the AC could be turned up. A few minutes later he asked if the AC could be turned down because he was too cold. Not long afterwards he was hot again. And so it went until around midnight, when he apologized for being a pain and asked why I didn't throw him off the boat.

"Oh, it's not a big deal," I said. "I don't even have an air conditioner on this boat. If you're hot it's because the wind's stopped blowing and if you're cold it's because it's picked back up again."

Despite my best efforts Pendo could not shake that powerboat mentality of getting on with the fun and getting on with it in a hurry. As you can guess, Pendo hasn't mentioned sailing since.

A few weeks later, I invited an old surfing buddy down for a weekend cruise. The Beaufort Yacht Club was sailing to Cape Lookout and I figured anybody who spent his days bobbing up and down in the breakers like displaced shark bait could handle a three-hour sail in the ocean, but the nice thing about experience is that you can recognize a mistake when you are making it again. We were barely out of the Beaufort Inlet when he became silent and lethargic. I asked him to pull in the jib sheet and he moved as if he were balancing a dish on his head. That's when I noticed his sunburned cheeks had faded to rose.

"Are you feeling alright," I asked.

"Uh, sure. I just got a mild case of the queasies," he replied. "It's probably from all those Becks last night."

As the wind and waves continued to build, I watched him clamp down on the cockpit coaming.

"Are you sure you feel okay?" I asked again.

"Oh, yeah, don't worry about me. I'll be fine as soon as we reach Lookout. How much further is it, anyway?"

"Four, maybe five miles."

"That far? I feel like we've been out here for days."

"Do you want to turn back?" I asked.

"Naaah. I'm okay. Really."

The fractured swells continued to build, so I reefed the main and fell off the wind.

"How much would it slow us down if I trailed along behind on my surfboard?" he asked at last.

"A lot. Look, Phil, we don't have to go to Lookout. We can turn around and go back to Beaufort if you like."

"Which is closer?"

"We're about halfway, but the ride back would be smoother," I offered.

"I hate to be a wiener," he said apologetically.

"I'd hate for you to barf all over my boat," I answered as we came about.

It is a credit to Phil that he never tossed his blueberry muffins to the fish, but that gutless feeling confined him to port for the rest of the weekend and relegated me to the role of babysitter. So now I'm back in the closet again and this time I'm staying put. It's safer in here. I know some will say entertaining guests is half the fun of yachting. Maybe it is for them, but not for a wimp like me. From now on, if a friend wants to go cruising, I'll direct him to the Moorings and wish him well. To paraphrase from the Gospel of Mark:

"The holy passion of Friendship is of so sweet and steady and loyal and enduring a nature that it will last through a whole lifetime, if not asked to go weekend sailing." Amen, brother Twain.

CREW *COMBA*TABILITY

"Waterfront Home For Sale; Two Bedroom, One Bath, Living Room, Kitchen & Porch with spectacular view overlooking the water. Owner anxious to sell. $35,900 or best offer."

It wasn't the ad's wording that caught my attention, so much as its placement in the publication. Had the advertisement sat dully amongst the other real estate properties, it would have garnered little interest, but there it was bold and direct in the middle of the "Boats For Sale" section of the Pamlico News. A clever enticement, I thought.

We followed the owner's directions and found the vessel lashed to a drooping finger pier at the end of a narrow creek. The bow line had slipped off the rotting planks and disappeared underwater. I was about to retrieve the errant rope from the mire, but the brown velvet growth coating the line changed my mind. A pool of shallow water in the cockpit supported a film of green algae and we were obliged to step carefully for footing on the seats as the drains were clogged with small leaves. A small forest of new pines were growing along the edge of the toe rail and I noted the owner had failed the first rule of boat selling——make the craft presentable. I began to mentally subtract dollars from the asking price.

The captain arrived with a rubbery bulge of fat overlapping the rim of his khaki slacks. A band of sweat encircled his waist, spreading down to his crotch. The pink flesh was stretched taut across his face and folds of weathered meat shielded his dusty brown eyes. Beads of perspiration glistened beneath the mat of thinning blond hair.

"It appears to be a nice design," I commented. "Why are you selling her?"

"The family has decided they don't like sailing anymore and I can't care for the boat alone."

"Ever sailed it offshore?"

"We took it to the Bahamas once. We were going to spend the summer cruising the islands while the boys were out of school, but that idea didn't last. My wife had suggested I install air conditioning and refrigeration before we left, but I protested. It didn't seem seamanlike. I should have compromised, but I was pig headed about the thing and insisted on having it my way. In hindsight, I guess I got what I deserved because it took about two weeks before the bugs and heat drove us home. I paid a guy to bring her back and we haven't used it much since. Once the dream was shattered, I lost all interest. Now I play golf. It doesn't require 'crew compatibility'," he said making no effort to hide his bitterness.

It happens like that sometimes. The husband has the idea he's going to quit his job and sail around the world with his family in tow. He sees himself cruising the islands on a micro-budget, teaching his children celestial navigation and self-reliance. The crew's diet consists of fresh lobster, grouper and coconuts. Air conditioning is a tattered bimini and ice is something they scrape off the roads in New York. Sometimes you'll read about a family like this that adapts to this impoverished lifestyle, but they are a rarity.

The story is played out on the shores of Georgetown and Ocracoke alike. Some embittered members call it crew *combat*ability and the husband is often the culprit. On the whole, men seem to dwell on the pressures and frustrations of life more than women. We think we've got the market cornered on stress and job repression and we wallow in our shallow puddle of self-pity, making the rest of the family miserable. Women enjoy these moments of romanticism, too, but they usually move on to the practicality of the idea and allow their good sense to hold their emotions at bay. They dream of adventure and tropical paradise but understand that long-range cruising costs money. Men, on the other hand, often neglect the fears and concerns of their family and demand confidence and skill instead. We ask for patience and trust, yet reward our crew with tirades and personal insults. People respond to kindness. They need to be praised and, often times, they need be pleased with themselves before they will listen to instruction. Most would agree it is more fun working for a boss who recognizes when a job is well done, but even when the crew fails, they deserve praise for trying. A good manager knows that a little kindness goes a long way and that is certainly true with cruising.

Make no mistake about it. Stuffing the family into a yacht for extended periods of cruising can be an interesting and rewarding way of life, providing everyone agrees on the basic necessities. Still, when the idea takes hold of their inner soul and the desire cannot be satisfied with weekend excursions, the couple will lay solid plans, ensure that they have adequate finances and take off—usually with excellent results. But sharing the same dreams is not always enough. To ensure safe passage, it requires crew compatibility as well. In the end, I liked what I saw. The boat would have made a splendid family cruiser, but we did not buy it. The wife indicated several features to which she objected—the lack of sitting head room in the V-berth, for one and her input is vital to our success. We each share the power of veto.

So, next weekend we'll look some more and with any luck, we'll find another near-sighted captain who's abandoned his boat. If the shouts on the docks are any indication, the market abounds with dreams for sale.

"The wife has decided she doesn't like sailing anymore and I can't care for the boat alone. Now I play golf. It doesn't require 'crew compatibility.'"

Barely Boating

"I swerved to miss the other car, then tried to hang on as my boat bucked along the highway like a Brahma bull. I glanced back in my mirror and saw the trailer rear up on one wheel. That's when I realized that I was about to go down with my boat... in the middle of the highway."

SHAKING LOOSE A ROLLING HITCH...HIKER

Last year was a good one for sailing, the best I can remember. I sailed almost every Wednesday night in the beer can races, participated in the Wachovia regatta from Wrightsville Beach to Morehead City and went to Ocracoke once. I sailed down to Beaufort a few times and the Bahamas twice. In between those excursions, I kicked around the docks at Whittaker Creek, rode my bicycle along the quiet streets of Oriental and helped skipper a Hunter thirty-something to a last place finish in the Fourth of July regatta on Lake Norman. All in all, last year was about the best ever. Why, I can't remember a year when I sailed as much or had as much fun doing it and I did it all on someone else's boat.

You see, I've become what is known around the docks as a "rolling hitch hiker," a moocher—a boat bum of the worst kind. Anyone in the boating industry will tell you last year was a bad year for selling a boat. Interest rates were high, credit was hard to get and many manufacturers found it easier to heave-to in bankruptcy court than beat against the winds of recession. Worst of all, prices in the used boat market plummeted as owners scrambled to escape with what little equity remained in their vessels. Yet, as bad as it was, I was out there trying to sell mine, just the same.

I listed it with the dealer, two yacht brokers, ran ads in all the major boating publications, slashed the price—twice, raised the broker's commission and offered to deliver the boat any place the new owner desired. A year and a half later, it's still for sale and on the trailer. Though other owners continued to sail while trying to market their yachts, my crew was not as fortunate. Our Nimble 20 was perfect for the wife and me when it was purchased, shrank a bit when our crew grew to three, then became completely out of the question when we our number reached four. In short, we ran out of boat before we ran out of crew and as a result of my careless procreation, the family did not have a suitable boat to use last season.

But I did because I went boat bumming. I worked my way into the starting lineup at the Oriental Wednesday Night Races and landed a job as grinder and bar tender on a Ranger 23. "Two Buds and half a turn on that winch," was my call to action. True, the crew performed better in my absence, but I attribute that feat to their sobriety since none of the crew could reach the cooler from their station. Having secured a ride for at least one day a week, the next task was to find some rest and relaxation on a large sailing vessel whose owner needed a crew of deck hands to coil the lines, tune the rig, polish the bright work, flake the sails and scrub the deck.

I found just such an individual one Monday last summer. After a quick trip down the waterway from Annapolis, the delivery captain presented the C&C 38 to its new owner at Whittaker Creek, commenting that the vessel was in great condition. As soon as he off loaded his gear and dirty laundry, our crew jumped aboard, backed out of the slip and headed for Ocracoke without so much as a deck wash. It was later that evening, as I steered for the soft ember of light off the Outer Banks, that I knew I had found my calling. I was a natural born boat bum.

I was visiting the in-laws on Lake Norman Fourth in July when the urge to go slow in a sailboat compelled me to amble over to the Lake Norman Yacht Club. The race committee had begun their skipper's meeting and with so many people milling around, I had little trouble talking my way onto a large Hunter sailboat. I have forgotten the skipper's name, but I remember he had this thing about his spinnaker sheets. We were dousing the chute after rounding a mark, when one of the sheets escaped and slipped over the side. The captain peered into the water as the red line sank out of sight, calculated the replacement cost and dove overboard, leaving the helm unattended. I'm not sure Warren Luhrs would have approved of the skipper's actions, but then, Warren probably gets his jib sheets for free. We abandoned the race, opened the bar and enjoyed the rest of the day immensely.

Last Spring, Captain George was looking for a warm body to stand the graveyard watch offshore as he prepared to bring his OC 40 home from the Bahamas. He offered me airfare to the Abacos, free food and drinks at the Conch Inn and the opportunity to do some blue water sailing.

"All I ask in return," he said, "is that you refrain from throwing up in the main salon. If you feel the urge to puke, go topside."

After the flight down, our crew assembled inside the heat of a 72' Bellaire station wagon and the driver whisked us away from Marsh Harbor International Airport, dodging craters in the broken asphalt as he carried us to Boat Harbour Resort on

Great Abaco Island. While the rest of the crew bought beer and provisions, I strolled up to the poolside deli to peruse the young vacationing wildlife and sample a bowl of conch fritters. Both proved spicy and baked to perfection—a just reprieve for the hours spent pressed between sweaty Haitians and surly Miami businessmen. Some people like their fritters plump and doughy with just a pinch of conch flavoring, but I'm not one of them. I like a chewy fritter with just enough bread to keep the meat cemented together in the golden nugget. I remember that batch was exceptionally good, as the cook added a dash of cheese flavoring to the breading. It made the warm St. Pauli Girl all the better.

Friday morning we sailed north along the chain of islands until a jammed centerboard forced us into the slings at Green Turtle Cay. We spent most of the day sanding the centerboard ram at Abaco Yacht Services under the competent eye of Everett Roberts, enduring the heat and tedious work with thoughts of a frosty Goombay Smash. When at last we finished our task and reached the Blue Bee Bar in the center of New Plymouth, we were crushed to learn that Ms. Emily had fallen into poor health and the bar was closed. We inquired of other taverns where one might get Goombay Smashed and were directed to the Rooster's Rest and Pub at the top of the hill. After drinks and dinner, Danny called me out for a game of basketball at the Green Turtle Recreation Center—a full court, green slab of concrete, complete with worn leather ball and chain nets. I was in my element and Danny, despite his superior quickness, could not match my outside shooting. That and I kept stepping on his bare feet.

Bright and early the next morning we were on our way to the "fish store" which was an island rumored to be the official base camp for all Spiny Lobster in the Abacos. Given the price of seafood dinners in the islands, I refused to believe catching lobster could be that easy, but I was wrong. Within the hour, we had filled both the bucket and floor of George's Avon dinghy with lobster and were still pulling them out two at a time. I dare say, there has never been a fresher lobster salad served than that which we enjoyed that first night at sea.

Later that spring I hitched a ride in the Wachovia Cup, went cruising with the Neuse Sailing Association over the summer, then sailed back to the Bahamas last November. I did some rough ciphering and figure I sailed more than 1,500 miles last year without ever stepping foot on my boat except to sweep the pine straw off the decks and pump the water out of the bilge. Not bad for a rolling hitchhiker.

But the free rides are over. My friends in the Bahamas brought the boat home without me this year and the Wednesday night gang has begun supplying me with listings from Soundings Magazine. One friend moved his boat to another marina. He won't say which one, but the message is clear. It's time I got a bigger boat.

So next weekend I'm going boat hunting in earnest. I have a chance to trade my Nimble 20 for a Ranger 33 and in this type of used boat market that may be my only hope of saving the dream. If the deal goes through, I'll name my new boat Friend-Ship in honor of all those comrades who kept me afloat last year. I figure it's the least I can do.

SMALL BOATS AND BIG HEARTS

The scuffed and tattered day sailer carved a silver row on the face of the slanting swell as the young skipper guided the slender craft towards the sloping beach, his confidence growing under the warmth of the August sun. He leaned back, shifted his weight towards the starboard quarter for balance and plunged through the surf, overtaking a faltering wave just as it began to crumble. The fickle dinghy surged over the white water as Jim, the young skipper, fought to maintain control. Slowly, the speed of the surf overwhelmed the force of the wind and the mainsail became limp, sagging lifeless on the boom. Young Jim, still seated along the rail, scrambled awkwardly towards the center of the craft to keep from falling in, but he was too late. The rowdy vessel spun around like a horse glaring back at its rider and broached in a tumbling explosion of foam, tossing the wild-eyed Jim across the rigging and into the surf. Jim groped for his wounded vessel in the shallow breakers around his knees until he found her. She had turned turtle; pitch-poled as they say, exposing the scars of other adventures on her battered center-board.

Slowly, young Jim realized the folly of his carelessness. He hiked up the port side of his craft, as if peeping under a bed sheet and studied the damage. The mast had been sheered off at the deck.

With great sweat and effort, Jim pulled his boat onto the beach and in his words, "circumcised the mast." He cut away the jagged base, returning the sturdy pipe to its original form. He replanted the mast, albeit shorter now and pushed his lady back into the surf. Within seconds, young Jim was carving a new path across the ocean's playground and the demasting was just another yarn to spin.

Jim Martin eventually married and became a father, a professor, a congressman and North Carolina's first two-term governor. Later, he would sail larger yachts across greater waters, but he would never forget the thrill of sailing that ragged day sailer, for such is the charm of a small boat.

I was recounting this story on one of those frigid, winter evenings, when my friend Rod denounced the boating industry in general and claimed they were spending all efforts selling to themselves. "Nobody cares about the little guy anymore," he declared. "Pick up any sailing magazine and count the number of advertisements you find for small day sailers. You'll be lucky to find one."

In fact, I found two. It seems small-boat manufacturers have decided it is not worth their time to advertise in "yachting" magazines, since the ad rates are high and the profit per unit sold low by comparison. The number of manufacturers who refuse to build a model under twenty-seven feet compounds the problem further. Granted, there are still a few who offer everything from a day sailer to an offshore cruiser, but their ranks are slim and thinning fast. It's a simple matter of mathematics, I guess. Why strive to please a hundred green-gilled first-time buyers when you can devote the same love and attention to one forty-foot yacht and make three times the money? So I agree the practice makes good business sense, but it strikes me as a short-term approach to a long-term problem. Like the farmer who spent his days polishing the apples while neglecting to water the roots, the boating industry may soon find it has starved the tree that feeds it.

New blood must be introduced if the boating industry is to survive and most marine publications share in the blame, because editors maintain their readers are more interested in a Pacific crossing to Bora-Bora than in a weekend excursion in the Chesapeake Bay. They forget that for most of us, it is not the length of the passage that matters, but the size of the adventure and the heart of the skipper. A trans-Atlantic crossing in a Valiant 40 and a jaunt down the Pamlico Sound in a ComPac 16 can both be life-changing moments with the right boat and wrong conditions.

I remember my first introduction to sailing. Bennie and I had combined our summer vacation money with another couple and purchased a well-worn, beet-red Snark sailboat. On a bright July afternoon we launched our yacht at the Morehead City public ramps and set sail for Beaufort. Our four hulking frames dwarfed the cozy cockpit, yet we still found room for a radio and a picnic basket. Because I had previous sailing experience—I had owned a windsurfer for a summer—I was appointed captain. I soon relinquished command, however, to Susan, the head of her household. It seems she had spent the previous weeks studying her Annapolis Book of Seamanship and whenever Kevin or I would suggest a correction in course, Susan would expose our ignorance and push on. We soon gave up and joined Bennie in silent prayer. Despite our bumbling efforts the spunky little craft zipped along nicely on a beam reach and soon we were approaching the old Atlantic Beach Bridge for its appointed opening.

We allowed the larger vessels to enter first and then followed, coming to an abrupt stop midway through as the huge concrete pilings blocked our wind. Against a brisk tidal current, we improvised and paddled our way through the opening until at last we cleared the bridge to the cheers and curses of those above.

Due to the length of our passage and our waning patience, we altered course and decided to make landfall at the Sanitary Fish Market on the Morehead City waterfront. We toasted our first passage with iced teas and hush puppies, slipped the lines and started back. The southwesterly winds were dying as we made our return approach to the swing bridge and with a twenty-minute delay until the next opening, we decided to see if we could slip under the bridge with our small rig. We almost succeeded, but the top of her mast butted the steel girder above. At last the bridge opened and we fell in behind the larger yachts as they motored through. This time, however, the bridge tender would have none of our antics. His siren gave a low growl and he closed the bridge. We came about slowly and drifted over to the Morehead City shore, where we dropped the mast and walked our lady under the bridge, rested a bit, then re-stepped the rig and sailed home.

It had been a triumphant day. We had sailed with the big boats and the lessons I learned sailing that tiny Snark have served me well as I have moved on to larger boats. That's why the current thinking among boat-builders bothers me. I fear many new sailors will jump right into boating and miss the opportunity to enjoy the raw excitement of small-boat sailing. Every seaman pays his dues at some point and experience is seldom a cheap education, but to miss the opportunity to learn on a small boat is to miss the tender years of a brooding dream. Skills and visions are polished like silver on those warm August afternoons on the water. Memories are born which last for life. I recall with fondness the advice of the owner who sold me the Snark.

"Study this boat and learn to sail her well," he said, "and never think of her as just a toy. With proper provisioning and experience, she can take you anywhere your heart desires—and if she doesn't, your dreams will."

TRAILER SAILOR SORROWS

I have this problem. Well, it's nothing, really. Hardly worth mentioning at all. Just a little something that flares up from time to time. Why, I wouldn't have brought it up at all except that it relates to boating. You see, it's really kind of embarrassing. I can't trailer a sailboat.

Believe me, I've tried. But you know how it is. Some of us have trouble anchoring, others docking. In fact, I've seen some who couldn't even get the sails up without wrapping them around the headstay. But when it's all said and done at least those folks are on the water. If you were not fortunate enough to witness their theatrics, you would think they were skilled sailors.

But I can't get in the water. Or if I do get in, I can't get out. It's been this way from day one. You'd think I would have learned the first time and given up by now. My wife, Bennie, wishes I had. There we were at the Wildlife ramp in Beaufort with my new (new to me, anyway) ComPac 16. I was going to spend the week cruising Core Sound and maybe go as far as Ocrakoke if weather permitted. I had her cleaned and provisioned and ready for a week-long shakedown cruise. Given that it was a sunny Saturday afternoon in the spring, things were kind of busy at the ramp, so the only available parking space was beside the tennis courts. Bennie and I got out, raised the mast, took the strap off and made sure everything was secure before I put the car in reverse. Backing a trailer has never been my strong suit and I was having a difficult time, what with the other cars and low-hanging tree limbs and all. In short, I finally backed myself into a corner. I looked around and realized the only way out was around the tennis courts. It was less crowded over there anyway.

I forgot about the telephone lines.

I never thought I'd forget a thing like that. Years earlier, a friend of mine had died when he lowered the mast of a Hobie 16 onto a power line, so it's one of those mental checks I always go through. Anyway, I forgot to check. I stopped at the road, looked left, then right and then pulled out. Something snapped and splintered and about that time the ground shook. All I could see in the rearview mirror was the blue hull of my new boat. The transom was crushed, as were my plans for the week. Oh well, you learn from your mistakes, they say.

I'm a slow learner.

The next incident was when the side-stay separated on the port turnbuckle as I was pulling her out of a gravel ramp. The landing had not been properly maintained, making it a very rough launch. Anyway, the mast fell to the side and bent the base plate, but I was lucky. It only cost me some pride that day. Oh well, live and learn, right?

There was still more to learn.

Next was the time I was trying to put her back on the trailer along the ICW when a 40-foot Bertram roared down the ditch pushing a three-foot swell. It was the biggest breaker I'd seen all summer. I knew I was in trouble when my buddy shouted out, "gnarly swell, dude," and jumped in with his surfboard. A moment later, my boat was sitting sideways on the trailer and the water was flowing back into the Waterway, leaving me hard aground...again.

Did I mention the time I almost sank the trailer? You see, we have one of those little compact cars and sometimes I can't get the trailer in far enough without drowning the vehicle. On those occasions I tie one end of a rope to the bumper hitch and the other end to the trailer tongue and have what my crew fondly calls a "controlled crash." When the boat has floated itself off, I pull the trailer out by the rope, chock the trailer tires and roll the car back to the hitch and reconnect my rig. It works very well.

On this particular day the water was low. Really low. We were beginning to talk of holding our own sandbar party if it dropped another foot. By the time the trailer was deep enough to float the boat, my rope was gone and so was my trailer. I threw Bennie the bow line and dove under, trying to find the tongue of the trailer. When I came out of the water empty-handed people were gathering along the shore to watch and offer assistance.

"Can I help you find something?"

"No. Thanks anyway."

"I'm real good at finding things in the water. What did you lose? A purse? A pair of sunglasses?"

"My trailer."

"Boat trailer?"

"Yeah."

"Well, that shouldn't be too hard to find."

"Yeah, it's not like it could have floated off or buried itself in the mud."

"How did it roll in? Trailer hitch come undone?"

"No, I unfastened it."

"Oh. Is this your first time out?"

"No, just the first time I've lost my trailer."

"Are you sure there's nothing I can do?"

"Well, you might tell those folks waiting to use this ramp that I'll get out of their way as soon as I find my trailer."

"Sure, I'll explain it to them…if I can."

It might have been that same trip when another car tried to run me off the road. The driver drifted across the centerline into my lane, so I swerved to miss him and then tried to hang on as my boat whipped me back and forth across the highway. I felt like a cowboy on a Brahma bull. I managed to grab a quick look in the mirror and saw the trailer up on one wheel and figured that was it. I was going down with my boat—in the middle of the Interstate A few miles later I pulled into McDonalds and found the bolts to the base plate were missing and the mast was ready to slide off. I shudder to think what might have happened if we'd really had our hearts set on that eight piece bucket of Kentucky Fried Chicken at the next exit.

As it is, I now suffer from a mental disorder called "Trailerphobia." On the advice of several authorities, my yacht broker for one and my wife for another, I've recently begun treatment for my ailments and put the *La Vie Dansante* where she should have been all along—in a slip. And that's where she'll stay until they bury all power lines, pave every boat ramp and rewire the mast so it can be raised and lowered with a garage-door opener.

There's just one catch. I have this problem. It's nothing big, mind you. Just a little something that flares up from time to time. In fact, it's hardly worth mentioning at all. You see, it's kind of embarrassing. I can't dock a sailboat.

But that's another story.

TRUE CONFESSIONS

Okay, I admit it. I'm an addict. Now don't get me wrong. I'm not a recovering addict or a reformed addict or even interested in getting help. The fact is, I kind of enjoy my habit. Bottom line? I'm a short cut junkie.

I just can't get enough of the little rascals. Given the choice between doing it by the book and doing it the quick and easy way, I'll take the short cut every time. I cut through neighborhoods to miss stoplights, put groceries back so I can use the express lane and disregard printed instruction sheets if they are more than a page long or printed in two languages. (What do manufacturers think? If I get confused in English, I'll understand it in Spanish? Just give me more pictures!)

I realize I'm not alone in my plight. Addiction is the polyester suit of the eighties—everybody is hiding one. People are hooked on chocolate, doughnuts, jogging, fishing, golf, ice cream, sex and M.A.S.H. reruns. None of which are chemical dependencies. The point is, this type of addiction is a mental disorder and often more difficult to kick. Or at least it is for me. Every time I try to kick one, it kicks me.

Of course, cutting corners is not always bad. In the business world, discovering a short cut can often save the company money. Which in turn may lead to a promotion. Which could mean you have found a short cut up the corporate ladder and should give yourself high marks. A double short cut is rare.

Short cut investing is also on the rise these days. As proof I give you the 1987 Stock Market crash, which wiped out many a young family's hope of circumventing the drudgery of long-term saving. Like so many before them, they were tempted by the short cut apple and they bit, proof that its deceptive powers cut through all social classes. For me, however, the sting of cutting corners is felt not in the Stock Market but on the water. Give me an approaching thunderstorm and a shoal-draft boat and I'll find a short cut back to the marina. I'll also find crab pots, submerged pilings, sandbars and oyster beds. You see, that's the problem with short cuts. Most of the time they aren't. This blinding revelation came to me while I was waiting for an incoming tide. I'd been coming back in between the channel markers and land and, well, suddenly I found this great spot for clamming.

My friends in Oriental claim I got just what I deserved. They say a short cut is the longest possible distance between two points and that I've traversed the Intracoastal Waterway enough to know better. I hate it when they're right. But I figure if a boating short cut is managed properly, it will give you more time on the water, fewer headaches and more beer money. At least that's the sales pitch of the boating industry. Next time you're around the docks, take a look at the number of sailboats that have roller furling, flaking mainsail, self-steering and Loran. With these amenities you can be ignorant and lazy and still be admired by all. I called it the Ronald Reagan approach to boating.

I had the opportunity to consider this phenomenon while surveying my new half-acre island and realized that my desire to cut corners is fueled by two factors. One, I hate waste and two, I got a bad case of lazies. I've always hated waste. I never throw anything away. I've got enough old newspaper clippings, books on sailing and *Cruising World, Sail* and *Coastal Cruising* magazines to keep the fireplace stoked all next winter. I hang on to disposable razors in case the new ones wear out. I have a lazarette full of five-foot-long dock line, an extra sail from two boats ago, more busted fenders than a Detroit crash site and a drawer full of old love letters from past sweethearts—like the razors, in case the new one wears out.

What I hate worse than anything is wasted time. The way I see it, short cuts save time, time is money and I never have enough of either. I've been lazy for as long as I can remember. I ride when I should walk. Sit rather than stand. Lie down whenever possible. And sleep if nobody is looking. Sometimes even when they are. I don't work out (it has that word in it). Not that I don't enjoy sports, mind you. I'll race a sailboat occasionally and I'll take a game of basketball anytime. But it's not really exercise if you top it off with a beer and a nap.

This laziness and hate for waste carries over into my boating. I seldom clean the hull or put on new bottom paint. It's easier to sell the boat. When I do dispose of the old girl, I strip her clean because the new owner will rarely give me more than a dime on the dollar for the extras I've added. Every time I trade boats, the yacht brokers tell me things like the teak grate and propane grill can't be figured into the selling price because the next owner may not care for them. Hey, I never took care of them either. I don't replace shackles or blocks or sheets or sails. Odds are the next owner won't appreciate my efforts anyway. Besides, then I'd have to find someplace to store all those discarded items and I'm overstocked with dock line and teak grates as it is.

I realize mine is a nearsighted approach. I've been told countless times that if it's not worth doing right, then it's not worth doing, so I don't do much. But I can't help myself. I'm a short cut addict. My wife says it's because I have no patience. If I wanted patience, I'd have been a doctor. I'll take short cuts instead.

In Harms Way

There ought to be a law against letting guys like me pilot a sailing vessel in the open water. At best, I'm a navigational hazard prone to strike any object that ventures near my bow or crosses my wake and at worst, I'm a threat to the health and safety of seamen everywhere. It would not surprise me greatly to learn that the Coast Guard had issued a directive requiring me to wear a sign across my chest, which read: *CAUTION! Un-abled bodied seaman at the helm. Approach at your own risk.* It's guys like me who are giving the rest of the sailing fraternity a bad name.

This honest assessment of my piloting skills might surprise some, though none who have ever sailed with me. The fact is, I needed to get this matter off my chest. That and the fact that I was tired of people talking behind my back. From now on, if you think I hogged the channel leading into the marina or refused to respect your right of way, just tell me to my face. It won't bother me a bit, because it's all true.

I felt obligated to announce my shortcomings now that I've moved up to larger sailboat. I bought that Ranger 33 I was telling you about, so I've expanded my sights to some new cruising grounds. My old Nimble 20, due to its restricted sail area and fuel capacity, limited the range of my destruction to the lower Neuse River area. Friends sailing out of Oriental knew to stay clear when the little green boat came meandering their way. Those on the docks took cover as I approached with a fender and dock line in hand. Quite frankly, I could only do but so much damage in that little boat, but now that I've moved up to a larger vessel I'm a real threat, so I've made a list of places I plan to visit this year—areas you will want to avoid.

Ocracoke. The harbor is small, the bottom notorious for poor holding and the dockage limited. Despite these restrictions, Ocracoke is the closest thing we have on the East Coast to Hopetown harbor in the Abacos. The anchorage is well protected and bordered by beautiful beaches, marine forest and an ancient lighthouse. The village offers an assortment of dining opportunities from pizza to gourmet selections at the Back Porch. The village exudes a certain Cape Cod ambience, peppered with pirate legends and a rich nautical heritage. I plan to visit the island a lot.

I have two anchors on board my new boat, but neither is in all that great a shape. The smaller one might be a dinghy anchor, but I can't be sure. The chain on the other is almost rusted through and the rope is too short. I'll probably anchor out, anyway, to avoid the tourists parading back and forth along the waterfront. I suggest you just get a slip. Best time to avoid Ocracoke? Late June and early July.

Cape Lookout. The holding is good, but crowds make me nervous and Cape Lookout is always crowded when I go. I've snagged at least one anchor rope while circling the parking lot looking for a space. I like to play my stereo loud and relieve myself off the back of the boat at night and this could prove annoying on a calm evening. Best time to avoid Lookout? Memorial Day weekend and anytime in September.

Bath. Back Creek splinters off Bath Creek towards the east and is over a half mile wide with good holding up to shore. On most summer afternoons, a thermal breeze fills in from the Pamlico River and funnels right up the creek, cooling the air just enough to make cocktails a poetic experience. Seasoned cruisers covet both Back Creek and "the Bay" dearly. I'd love to anchor out, but if it looks crowded I'll try to tie up at the town docks.

I usually try to pick a space with plenty of room on either end, but I can't control such things—or my boat when docking most times. I tend to bounce off the pilings when I bring her in, ram the bulkhead, then stop. It isn't pretty, but we haven't lost anyone yet. Sometimes I miss and slide over into the next slip. I wouldn't want the boat in the neighboring slip. Better avoid Bath in July and August.

Beaufort. The current is wicked, the crowds on the dock noisy and the anchorage is congested in season. I usually arrive in Beaufort with a bang. I've crashed into the dock twice, run aground once trying to anchor at night and drug anchor at least three times. Call it a curse, but Beaufort brings out the worst in my piloting skills. Still, I like its charms, so I sail down there every chance I get. I'm likely to show up most anytime, so I suggest you scratch Beaufort from your cruising list altogether.

Southport area. I want to spend some time kicking around Bald Head Island and Southport this summer, but I don't know when I'll be through. You'll just have to take your chances.

Manteo. I want the kids to see the "Lost Colony," and visit Fort Raleigh and the Elizabeth II. Bennie will probably want to stroll through the Elizabethan Gardens and I'll insist on at least one mug of freshly brewed Bavarian beer at the Weeping Radish. I'll probably wait until late summer or early fall, so June and July are pretty safe months for visiting Roanoke Island—unless the wind is right and we run up there from Ocracoke.

New Bern. I plan to be there for the Fourth of July fireworks. I'll anchor out, of course.

In looking back at this list, I realize I've roped off some pretty nice cruising areas for myself. If this seems selfish on my part, so be it. That's the way I am when it comes to summer cruising—greedy and ruthless. Of course, you can always take your chances and come cruising with me. I guarantee you'll enjoy the show, though I wouldn't recommend a front-row seat. I suggest you stay at least two boat lengths away; four is better. And who knows? With luck, encouragement and stern coaching from worried slipmates, I might learn how to drive this dang boat before the summer's out.

But don't count on it.

HARD AGROUND...AGAIN

A former college buddy stopped by my slip the other day and asked me a tough question.

"Jones, how did you do it? How did you get a job that allows you to spend the days anchored off the beach of some remote island, sampling rum punch and native women while getting paid to write about your sailing misfortunes?"

I looked up from my teak work and grunted, giving him a blank stare. "I haven't the faintest idea what you're talking about but if you can find me that job, I'd love to have it. I've been searching for that rhumbline all my life."

If my head had not been clouded from the demise of a St. Pauli Girl, I might have seized the chance and played a little Tom Sawyer—swapping his fresh enthusiasm for my tired, worn-out column—and we'd have both been better off for it. You see, I've been having a bad week this summer and the *Hard Aground* column is most of the problem. I need a reprieve—a vacation of sorts. Understand, it has nothing to do with you. I like you. I like the work. And I like meeting new people with strange and bizarre sailing adventures. They have more than made up for the slow days when my creative mind has stuffed its duffle bag full of floral print shirts, mini bottles of Tanqueray gin, toothbrush and Jimmy Buffett tapes and slipped off to some imaginary island, leaving me to face the bleakness of an imposing deadline.

And it's not like I'm overworked. I may be overextended on my credit cards, over budget on my boat fund and oversexed if you were to believe Bennie's comments, but overworked? That is not a problem. The hours aren't bad—I make my own. My publisher and editor are generous with their liquor and lodging and friendship. And the pay is adequate for the effort involved. All in all, I got it pretty good. So what's the rub?

I've become a prophet. A self-fulfilling one. And I can't stand the heat on the mountain. I have noticed that too many people are beginning to recognize me from my posture on the water. At first it was flattering to be noticed, then a little embarrassing, but now it has become all too frequent. Boaters sailing past a derelict washed up in the marsh slow their forward speed and holler out.

"Yo, Ed. Eddie Jones. Is that you over there?"

"Who else?"

"What are you doing? Building a duck blind?"

"No! I ran aground."

"Well, I can see that. But how? You're a good fifty yards from the channel."

"Never mind how. Just throw me a line."

"Are you kidding? I'm not about to let you pull me up there too!"

And so it goes until I'm hoarse from shouting and a fleet of busybodies has gathered to gawk at the spectacle. It wasn't meant to be like this. The column was intended to provide comic relief while waiting for life's tide to turn—thus the name, *Hard Aground*. Lord knows, if we mourned every squandered or bungled moment, life would be miserable indeed. So I take two aspirin, lay back and try to enjoy it. I call it the Bobby Knight approach to stress. But as I mentioned before, the column has become a self-fulfilling prophecy.

The first time was harmless enough. I was enjoying the use of a small day sailer and plowing a few rows in a nearby sandbar when I suddenly planted the centerboard. Hard. I tossed out my crew, told her to push and then continued on, minus the backseat navigation. As I remember, the day improved considerably. The next grounding occurred while loading a ComPac 16 onto its trailer at Holden Beach. A 40-foot Bertram roared down the ditch, pushing a three-foot swell into the next county and dropped my vessel sideways on the trailer. It looked worse than it was, but I was beginning to notice a pattern. Then there were some anxious moments in the channel over at Cape Lookout when we stuck hard under full sail with a gale building. Fear and panic roused the crew into action and we recovered quickly, but I was beginning to fear I was destined for fame and misfortune.

And then there was Camp Don Lee.

I had sailed down from New Bern in my Nimble 20 for a work weekend at the camp. The trip down was a classic run with a northwest wind on the stern and all three sails trimmed out nicely. Any other weekend the front would have clocked around and been out of the east or south by Sunday, but not this weekend. When Sunday afternoon rolled around, it was still blowing out of the northwest and I was not prepared for a beat home against the wind and current, so I received permission from the camp director to tie up to the canoe dock at the creek. All was quiet when I left that Sunday afternoon, but later that week I received a phone call from my friend Dave Edwards.

"Eddie, the first thing I want to say is that near as I can tell there's nothing wrong with your boat. At least, there aren't any scratches or holes in it that I can see. But then, the way she's sitting, it's hard to tell."

"What do you mean, the way she's sitting?"

"Well, she's resting on top of the canoe dock."

"You mean at the dock," I said correcting him.

"No, I mean *on* it. You'd better get over here and take a look."

On the way over I recalled hearing about a northeaster that had blown all week, filling up the lower Pamlico Sound and Neuse River. They had reported water in the streets of New Bern and a car had been blown from the bridge. When I drove into camp, I could see *The Captain and The Kid* sitting cockeyed on the pier. I asked camp director John Farmer what had gone wrong.

"Well, when the creek started rising, we pushed her away from the dock and anchored her out. We checked at the height of the storm and everything seemed to be in order. When the wind switched and the creek subsided, I guess she swung on her hook, because she floated over the top the dock and settled as the water dropped."

"Does it flood like this often?" I asked.

"I haven't seen it this high in over twelve years."

Twelve years! And I was only there one week. The good news is that with the help of the Camp Don Lee Sailing Staff, we got my boat off and she's now resting comfortably in Oriental, but my nerves are shot. I can't take any more of this. I'm afraid to go home on Sundays for fear I'll return to find her atop the Oriental bridge. So if you want to swap places with a haggard columnist for a few weeks, let me know. The brightwork needs cleaning, the deck and hull could use a good scrubbing and the salon needs varnishing. You write and work and I'll laugh at you for a while.

And if she asks, I'll tell Aunt Polly it was your idea.

BARE*LY* BOATING

It was one of those ideas that came to me while a cold January rain fell outside and I sat relaxing in the soft glow of a warm fire. I had a glass of Harris Teeter wine in one hand and my wife's *Southern Living* in the other and there, spread before me, was this advertisement for Florida's West Coast. In the background was the blue turquoise water of the Gulf stretching towards

Mexico, broken only by the parting wake of a white sailboat slipping south. In the foreground, the orange glow of the setting sun highlighting the pink palace outline of the Don Caesar hotel. Well, I thought, I've got some vacation money stashed aside and we have enough sailing experience that we could con our way onto a bare-boat charter.

"What do you think, dear? How's 80 degrees and sunshine sound to you," I asked Bennie. "Right, I'll call the airlines and you pour us another glass. We've got some planning to do."

So off we went dreaming of love and lobsters and secluded coves embroidered with Banyan trees and mangroves. I envisioned an anchorage where we could take an early morning dip, then recline with a Bloody Mary and chart the day's course over bagels and cream cheese. I saw myself sipping cold Becks under the bimini and listening to Buffett as we pulled up to the dock of Pete's restaurant on Anna Maria Island. You know, the kind of sailing I'm accustomed to here in the Carolinas.

I'm tempted to continue with this saga and explain how the markings in the channel didn't match those on the furnished charts. How the sun was also on vacation that week and we were blessed with gale force winds. How the charter company moved its location the week before we arrived…without telling us. But I figure, why spoil your dreams of chartering along Florida's West Coast just because I happen to be afflicted with terminal stupidity and bad luck? Still, if there is one lesson I learned during that week of chartering, it's that bare-boating is not intended for the enjoyment of the captain and crew. It might be a test of manhood or a ritual of religion, but enjoyment? Never!

The next time I want peace and pleasure, I'll check into the Don Caesar.

No, if chartering is to be enjoyed at all, it must be savored as a spectator sport—an event for the armchair captain, if you will. A sideshow for every yacht broker, yard dog, sail maker and dockhand located within walking or shouting distance of a marina. It must be so or else those folks would mind their own business and leave us alone. But they don't.

Or at least they didn't leave Bennie and I alone. As soon as they saw that a new bare-boat captain was in their marina, everyone ceased their activities, went below to wash up and announced on Channel 16 that a new skipper was in slip 12. Within minutes our nosey neighbors emerged scrubbed and dressed in their best nautical attire, with a fresh martini in one hand and canvas deck chair in the other and there I stood half naked in the cockpit of a Hunter 33, calculating the bacterial levels of the foul water beneath our hull. There was a little problem with one of the stern lines that required an up-close inspection of the prop. My pasty white rolls hung over the edge of my red shorts, sweat dripped off the end of my nose and my sunglasses were steaming up from humidity. Worst of all, there wasn't a beer opener anywhere on the boat. I was tempted to pack it in and fly home when a kindly gray-headed fellow strolled over and asked if the engine would crank. It did.

"What gear were you in when the line got tangled?" he asked.

"Reverse," I replied.

"Then put it in forward for just a moment and see if it breaks free."

It did and I thanked him, wondering why I hadn't thought of that.

"Don't mention it. Happens all the time down here. You were lucky. Most of 'em usually end up having to take the plunge anyway."

"So this type of thing isn't unusual," I asked.

"Gosh no. Not with bare-boaters. In fact, some of us have talked about moving to other marinas with better facilities and more protection, but those places don't allow charter companies. We'd miss all this fun if we moved."

"That's kind of sick, don't you think? I mean, getting your laughs at the expense of a fellow sailor."

"Listen, we're not as bad as those old timers over there in that retirement building. They'll give up lunch just to come over and place bets on how many times a bare-boater runs aground on that shoal out there. We live-aboards figure it's our just reward for having to maneuver around you guys when you get stuck in the channel or bang into our boat or throw a party at three in the morning because you're on vacation and we're not. Besides, you'd do the same if you had the chance."

"Never!"

"C'mon now. You mean to tell me you've never poked fun of bare-boater before?"

"I might have once or twice," I confessed. "But never again. Not after this week."

"You say that now, but just wait until you get back home. Now that you've paid your dues, why should you make it any easier on the next guy?"

"Yeah," I thought. "Why should I?"

I was tempted to embrace this sort of fraternal hazing and join in the fun when the next bare-boater tried his luck before the crowds along the Beaufort waterfront. I was tempted, that is, until I noticed something peculiar about that skipper and others in the marina. They didn't sail. Or at least they didn't go sailing while I was there. It seems the conditions were never just right. It was too windy or too cold or too late in the day. Then it rained, which made the next day's sunshine too hot, especially since the wind was dying.

All the time, Bennie and I were sailing every day and having a grand time, despite the lousy weather and leaking boat. And we weren't alone. I noticed other bare-boaters enjoying themselves, as well. I'm not saying those armchair captains weren't good sailors. I'm quite certain they could have tacked circles around me had they left the cozy confines of their slip. But they didn't.

So I've scrapped the notion of razzing bare-boaters. I doubt I'd have made a good fraternity brother anyway. Instead I have a new respect for bare-boaters. At least they are willing to take a chance and try new areas and different boats. That week of chartering reminded me that experience is what you get when you are looking for something else—that adversity adds seasoning to our character. So this summer, why not take some of that vacation money you have been saving and charter a yacht? Or if you own a boat, rent a larger one and expand your cruising range. Don't worry about how you'll look or whether you can handle it. Chances are you'll do just fine.

But make sure you pack a spare bottle opener…just in case.

"At least we're not as bad as those old timers over at the retirement center. They'll stop putting practice just to come over and place bets on how many times a bareboater will run aground in our channel."

Sailsmanship

*"What's a little corner-cutting among friends? This is
supposed to be a beer can race, right? If you busybodies think
I've been cheating, sue me. Otherwise, pass the beer pitcher.
I'm thirsty."*

SPRING COMMISSIONING THE SKIPPER

After a few false starts, spring has finally sprung and along with the pollen comes a rite of passage I dread even more than the hay fever: spring commissioning. Oh, I always begin with plenty of eagerness and zeal, but the motivation and skin on my knuckles usually wear off about the same time. I freely admit spring commissioning a sailboat is not my area of expertise. Lord knows, there are plenty of good articles that will reveal more than you care to know of the cancer that attacked your vessel this winter while you sat watching evening game shows and daytime soap operas and getting fat. Which brings me to an aspect of sailing that has long been neglected by the sailing authorities: spring commissioning of the captain.

Often we spend good time and money preparing the boat for another fun-filled season and forget about our own bodies. The first warm weekend in April and we're out with the Joy and a deck brush, washing the deck, caulking the leaks with epoxy and replacing busted hardware. But have you taken a gander at your own underside lately? Those little pockets of fat aren't blisters, I'll promise you that. It's no wonder the boot stripe sinks out of sight when you step aboard.

So this year I want to pass along some tried and tested tips for commissioning the captain. It's time to pour into our Land's End sailing shorts, alert the Coast Guard of our intentions and whip this crew into shape. First, let's exercise the mind—become mentally prepared for the challenges ahead. To do this go find yourself a brick wall on a crowded sidewalk and stand before it with an air indifference. Try to relax. Maybe tie your shoes a few times, glance at your watch, wave at the folks passing by if you like. But don't lose sight of the objective. Every so often turn back towards the wall and scowl as if you are ready to pounce upon it. This drill should prepare you for those long waits at the ICW bridges when they've changed the opening times to every hour on the half-hour until 9 AM, top of the hour until 12 AM and every other hour on the hour until the new bridge is completed or hell freezes over. If you spend much time sailing around the Wrightsville Beach area, stand before the wall and beat your head against, as well.

To prepare the lungs, I suggest you drive to a small country crossroads and find an old two-pump gas station that has one of those "COLD BEER SOLD HERE" signs lit up in the window. March inside and ask the owner if you may borrow his facilities. If he hesitates, tell him you'd also like a cup of fishing worms and a six-pack of Budweiser. Enter the restroom, pull the door closed and inhale slowly through your nose. Small puffs at first, building to long drags, until you can swallow several gulps of air at a time without losing your breakfast in the sink. This will prepare your lungs for those stormy nights at sea when you are at least a day away from any facility, the head is backed up and one or more of your crew had Dinty Moore baked beans for dinner.

Next is a stretching exercise. Go stand on a dock and have someone throw tennis balls just outside your reach. The object is to catch the ball without falling in. Your improved coordination will come in handy when you've run aground (again) and are faced with the embarrassing choice of either catching the tow line of a well-meaning but unskilled bare-boat captain or calling the Coast Guard for a tow. A third choice is to announce loudly for all to hear; "I thought we'd never arrive. Drop the anchor, honey and bring me another cold one."

Another favorite of mine is a good old game of tug-a-war, with a few variations. Instead of rope, use an old John Deere tractor chain covered with mud. Rather than pulling against another partner, fasten the bitter end to a sturdy iron fence and pull from the deep-squat position. This will build upper-body muscles and increase your chances of pulling up an anchor caught on that underwater cable not mentioned in the cruising guide.

A simple game of catch can be turned into a great reflex drill. Have three of your closest enemies stand a few feet in front of you with an ample supply of canned goods. Now, have each of them throw cans at you—slowly at first, until your reflexes improve from the beating. As you begin to catch a few cans, have your friends throw harder and faster. The game is over when you cover your head and cower on the floor. The cat-like reflexes you develop will be of great use when the cabinets in the galley are left unlatched and the helmsman gybes without warning.

These simple but important exercises will improve your physical condition and prepare you for another summer of fun-filled cruising. This year, don't bother with getting the boat in shape. Have some yard dog at the marina do all the messy stuff. This spring, spend some time on yourself and remember, no pain, no gain. From here on out it's sooth ailing.

BEER CAN RACING

The Oriental Association for Racing and Pillaging was concluding its Sunday afternoon Beer Can Regatta, which races on Wednesday and two by two, the merry mix of yacht brokers, sail makers and live-aboard vagabonds swaggered into the Trawl Door Restaurant, suffering from starvation and a severe case of bottle fatigue. Fierce competition and light airs had pushed emotions to the edge and the robe of sportsmanship had been trampled underfoot amid the crewmembers' petty bickering. The shouting and name-calling rumbled throughout the fractured brick halls and when the noise threatened to spill over into the main dining area, Thomas, our bartender, rose from his stool, pounded a beer bottle on the counter and herded the crowd off to the solitude of the banquet room amid the cheers and applause of the other patrons. Once sequestered, the verbal attacks continued.

"How dare you claim you beat us to the mark when you couldn't even see the piling? We were blocking your view with our bow."

"You weren't just shielding the mark, Danny dear, you were blotting out the whole stinking sky! You should give that floating half-acre of waterfront property to the Cherry Point Air Station to use in low-level bombing exercises. Either stay clear of our vessel at the finish, or I'll petition to have the *Jandivina* classified a navigational hazard."

"You're just sore because you called mast abeam and we ignored you. Anyone knows you can't call mast abeam until you're alongside the other boat. Hell, your bow was barely even with our stern."

"Oh, get real," Sue snapped, pulling her fork from its red napkin sheath. "We had right-of-way at the mark and you know it."

"Stop waving that fork in my face. And even if you had right-of-way, you can't fall down on the leeward boat and force him off course."

"Why not?"

"Because the rules say you can't!"

"Since when did you start racing by the rules? This is beer can racing. There aren't any rules. Just ask Jay. He hasn't rounded a mark all summer."

"Hold on, now," Jay said, looking up from his menu. "Don't go dragging me into your little spat."

Wally dabbed a wisp of beer foam from his mustache and leaned over. "I'm afraid she's got you there, buddy. You do have a knack for coming up short of the mark."

Jay shrugged. "So what's a little corner-cutting among friends? This is supposed to be a beer can race, right? If you busybodies think I've been cheating, sue me. Otherwise, pass the beer pitcher. I'm thirsty."

The subject was dismissed, another round ordered and the evening continued without incident, just as each of the previous Wednesday nights had ended with harmless hazing and good-natured ribbing. I thought about this exchange on the way home the next day as I tried to justify my participation in Wednesday night racing. My wife, Bennie, had insisted I explain why I felt it necessary to slip off in the middle of the week to race sailboats when I had previously declared my disgust for yacht racing.

"If it were another woman, I could understand," she said. "Not tolerate, mind you, just understand. But sailboat racing?"

"This isn't like what you see in the America's Cup. It's not really racing."

"Then what is it?"

"More like cruising in the fast lane."

"Aren't you trying to win?"

"Well, sure, but the main thing is to have fun and sail the boat to its potential. That's why everyone starts at the same time, regardless of boat length, make, or rating. Some days the conditions favor the small boats. Other days, when it's blowing a gale, the larger boats walk away. But everyone is trying to get the most out of themselves and their boat and that's what makes it fun."

"So who wins?"

"The first across wins, but that's not the point. The fact is, we all win, because the competition makes us better sailors."

"Sounds like the people in charge of that America's Cup thing could take a lesson from your Wednesday night crowd."

She's right, I suppose. It could be that the founding fathers of the America's Cup envisioned a friendly beer can race between competing nations, with the trophy and bragging rights the only real rewards. How they must cringe when they see what the harlot money and her huckster partner, television, have done to their beloved regatta. It's enough to make Sir Thomas Lipton spew his afternoon tea across the nav station.

The America's Cup charade is not unique, however. The lust for money and fame has defiled amateur and professional competition alike. Coaches no longer manage a team; they baby-sit millionaire athletes because they understand it's the players who put the fannies in the seats. If Michael Jordan tells the front office he's tired of playing for Doug Collins, then Mr. Jordan gets a new coach and Collins gets a new career. When it comes to yacht racing, it's the corporate sponsors who provide the revenue for the popular regattas and though this influx of money enhances sailboat technology, it does so at a price. The promise of corporate sponsorship increases the pressure to win and if that means stuffing the burgee of sportsmanship into a damp hanging locker and slamming the door shut, so be it. It seems over these past few months I've seen more of Sail America's legal team than I have of Dennis Conner's foredeck crew.

It wasn't always this way. A few generations ago we told our children that sportsmanship was to be valued above all else. "It's not whether you win or lose, but how you play the game," my Little League coach had to keep reminding us. We wanted to win at all cost, but we *needed* to learn how to play fairly. Nowadays, kids are encouraged to win by any means and bend every rule. If it is true that our youth learn by example, then we have every right to fear the future, for it's a safe bet that the next generation will show little mercy for those of us who play by the rules and can't keep up.

That's why I enjoy beer can racing so much. It revives those childhood memories where differences where settled on the ball field with swift and fair decisions. As a kid we all understood that the longer we stood around arguing about who was safe or out, the less time we had to play. Simple sportsmanship prevailed. One team would get the call this time and the other team would get it the next. If little Johnny didn't like the verdict, he could take his ball and go home. We could always find another ball and continue play, but it wasn't as easy for Johnny to find another game. In the case of the Wednesday night gang, we could each take our boat and go back to our slip when we felt we'd been wronged, but then we wouldn't have an excuse to drink beer and argue about the outcome of a race that means almost nothing in a town that offers so few diversions in the middle of the week.

So I guess I'll tell Bennie that doing almost nothing in Oriental on a Wednesday night with friends is more fun than doing almost anything else at home by myself. That should help clear up the matter.

MONEY PYTHON AND THE HOLY RUB RAIL

I was sitting out by the Dock House the other day, caressing a St. Pauli Girl as the *La Vie Dansante* thrashed about on her lines, when a friend of mine glanced up from his sailing magazine and asked, "Jones, what would you do if you had twelve million dollars?"

"The first thing I'd do is buy that powerboat captain a pair of reading glasses and direct him back to the NO WAKE sign. Then I'd have another beer. Why?"

"Well, you're one of those sailor types, so maybe you can help me understand this stuff. Why would a group of sailors go begging for money like some televangelist and then waste it all on some silly race? I mean this guy Dennis Conner has raised more than twelve million dollars so he can enter his boat in this America's Cup thing and what does he get if he wins? A car, a vacation? No way. He gets a cup. A trophy. And he doesn't even get to keep that. Some yacht club out in California gets the thing. So tell me, Jones. What's the deal with these guys?"

I'm the first to admit I don't know much about yacht racing and its participants. About the only time I move with any speed on a sailboat is when I find water seeping up through the cabin floor and remember the boat doesn't even have a bilge pump, manual or otherwise. Even then I take time to finish my beer. No point in being wet and sober. But lately I've found myself taking a curious interest in the upcoming America's Cup Challenge. For instance, I'm curious to know how the people of Chicago could move the whole town from Illinois and relocate it on the Atlantic. I'm interested to see how Tom Blackhaller's forward rudder will perform "down under" and I'm wondering if Dennis Conner will have a diet named after him now that he's shed 50 pounds of baby fat. Remember how overweight he was in '83 when he lost?

My buddy's question started me thinking about the America's Cup and wondering if it really reflects sailboat racing as most of us know it. And the more I read of the upcoming race, the more I'm convinced it does not. I mean, take this Chicago thing. Everyone knows Chicago is in Illinois and it sits on Lake Michigan. But the Chicago Yacht Club wanted to be in the race so badly, they argued that Lake Michigan was an arm of the Atlantic and therefore a "seaside city." Imagine telling someone you are from Chicago, a quaint little coastal village a little west of Newport. Our fair town of Charlotte sits on Lake Norman, which feeds the Catawba River, which eventually deposits its gallons into the Charleston harbor, but you haven't seen the Lake Norman Yacht Club organizing a syndicate. Not that they couldn't put together a first rate crew. We just understand when a halyard is being stretched a bit too far.

And what is the problem with the sailboat *French Kiss?* The IYRU executive committee has ruled that the French entry violates Rule 26, which prohibits any connection between a sponsor and the boat's name. The major sponsor is the company KIS FRANCE. Picky, picky, picky! Sounds like the kind of thing my mother might object to, though on different grounds, of course. You can bet if it was that bunch from Wrightsville

Beach sailing the boat, they'd rearrange that name to reflect their opinion of both the French and the executive committee. And my mother still wouldn't approve of the boat name.

If there is one central theme running through all the syndicates it is reflected in Dennis Conner's "Sail America" campaign and "sell America" is exactly what he's doing. The America's Cup has become big business on Madison Avenue and the message to the corporate sponsors from the syndicates is clear. You scrub my hull and I'll scrub yours. It wouldn't surprise me to see Lee Iacocca standing on the bow of the *Stars and Strips* shouting, "If you can find a better syndicate in America, buy it!" Which is exactly what has happened to America's Cup racing. Of the proposed 67.5 million dollars budgeted for the U.S. challengers, they have raised enough so far to buy 12 Pearsons, 25 Elites, 100 J-27s, 100 Beneteaus, 75 Hunters, 31 Cheoy Lees and 4500 Hobie Cats. It's enough to make a poor captain with a busted bilge pump cry. Of course, it's hard to keep all those sponsors happy without sacrificing a little self-esteem. Poor Dennis might be more formidable now that he's been seen driving around downtown Honolulu in a K Car with a backseat full of empty Bud cans. On the other hand, sponsorship agrees with Dennis's counterpart, John Kolius, who can be found tooling around the badlands of Australia in his new GM-furnished Cadillac, singing the Amway fight song, "This suds for you."

Then there are the politics and this time it's from the man who lambasted the New York Yacht Club for their high handed methods back in '83, Tom Blackaller. It seems Tom designed and built a boat with a forward rudder before the rule was changed to allow such a design. Why would he gamble the syndicates' money unless he was sure the rules would be changed to accommodate his new configuration—which it was. The lure for Blackaller and all the syndicates is, you guessed it, M-O-N-E-Y. A study performed by the Chapman College estimated the economic benefit to the winning syndicate's city to be one billion dollars. That's quite a nice piece of change for some lucky town, but if the average yacht club had any hopes of challenging for the cup, this year's extravaganza has put those dreams to rest. The Yale Corinthian Yacht Club and their boat are the only entry in the race that even remotely resembles a club-sponsored yacht. Theirs is a boat as numbered in years as it is long in meters and perfectly willing to challenge the money crowd for the Holy Grail. If the YCYC could win it all, then there would still be hope for the little guy. There would still be the chance to dream—a chance for some future Morehead City-Beaufort Yacht Club entry to take home the Cup.

And wouldn't it be nice to see Walter Cronkite standing in front of the Dock House, with a gentle breeze bringing in the last of the spectators from the course? Drinks would be flowing freely from the bar and the whole world would be focused on tiny Beaufort, NC, as Walt signed off; "So from the shores of North Carolina, where the Americans will once again defend their cup, I'm Walter Cronkite saying, so long for now. And that's the way it is."

And the way it should be.

TICK-TAX-(MY) DOUGH

You wouldn't know it from looking at me, but I'm part of the "new rich"—a recent pledge member of the upper crust, though I lean more towards the flaky than the dough side of the shell. Just the same, I am gratified with the manner in which I have made my fortune. My family was never a part of the establishment, so I've worked hard to get where I am. Just how did I come into this sudden wealth?

It happened overnight.

The seed was planted when I purchased my last sailboat. That was the beginning of my good fortune. Though few would consider the purchase of a sailboat as a prudent business venture, that modest feat enhanced my social status and provided me with the necessary credentials to join the ranks of the rich and famous. As of January 1, 1991, the U.S. Government now recognizes Eddie Jones as a card-carrying member of the group known simply as "the rich." Congratulations. You're in it too!

We all know who the rich are, or, at least we thought we knew. They were the ones with all the money. Malcolm Forbes is rich. Donald Trump used to be. Uncle Sam is not and never was, but he wants to be real bad, so he and his cronies in Washington amended that definition of "rich" to include anyone who owns a boat. One might assume I would be pleased with this honor, but I am not. Being a member of "the rich" involves club dues, $35 a year in my case. Hence, I would like to offer my resignation and ask that my name be withdrawn from the club's roster. I know what rich is. I have some friends who are. Trust, Mr. President, I'm not it.

Under the new law, all boat owners are to be taxed for the privilege of sailing on weekends. It is called a user fee, though there are no plans to spend the money on improved boating facilities or updating waterway charts. This generous contribution is intended simply to reduce the federal deficit. I'm feeling patriotic already.

I wouldn't mind the new law so much if I thought it would do some good, but it won't. Doing away with bureaucrats and special interest groups would help. Frugal spending on the part of these same bureaucrats would help even more. They could start by eliminating the $100,000 study on the sexual preference of the Japanese quail. What is there to know? Some birds like boys. Others like girls. Those who mate with members of their own sex have fewer offspring and are often found rearranging the feathers of fellow birds. Big deal.

Another way to cut spending and raise revenue would be to abolish the absurd practice of paying grown men not to do something or grow something on their land. If a man in Kansas has a knack for growing wheat, let him have it, but don't pay him good money NOT to grow wheat. I freely admit this suggestion may lack merit with some of my farming buddies, but it makes more sense than hurling another tax hike at the boating industry. We sailors already pay more than our fare share of taxes. Take my boat for example. There were numerous duties and import taxes attached to the goods used in the manufacturing process. A social security tax on the workers who built the boat and a sales tax when the boat was first purchased. I pay a fuel tax on every gallon I consume, a state registration tax and a county property tax at the end of the year. It's a wonder the bloody thing floats with all those taxes weighing it down.

But I am a patriotic American, so I'd be willing to help reduce the deficit, provided the new law taxed all forms of recreation. But why pick on sailing? What makes us different from say, a golfer or a league of bowlers? Consider how much revenue the government would collect with a 25-cent tax on all bowling shoe rentals or a nickel tax on the sale of new golf balls. It doesn't sound like much, I know, but I gather from this latest round of tax increases that our congressmen are desperate for revenue in any form.

Of course, the reason boating is singled out is because sailors are an odd bunch. People who don't own boats cannot understand us and what people do not understand, they attack. It has been this way throughout the ages. Land-kind has always enjoyed a nervous camaraderie with mariners. Seaman returning from foreign ports brought exotic wares and strange accounts from remote lands. The townspeople enjoyed the tales of adventure, but were careful not to give these vagabonds too much influence for fear they would lead their youth astray with wild hopes of fortune and fame, thus disrupting the fragile society of the cave dwellers. Our swashbuckling ancestors were kept on a short dock leash, you might say.

Nothing has changed.

If you tell someone you spent your vacation playing golf in Florida, they'll ask how you played and inquire as to the condition of the course. Tell 'em you're flying to Nassau to cruise down to the Exumas and they'll ask you what for.

"Why not just check into the Merv Griffin hotel on Paradise Island and relax," they'll ask.

"Because we want to go sailing."

"So take a cruise ship. Listen, I've got a friend who works at a travel agency and she's got this great package deal. It includes golf, casinos, entertainment and more food than you could eat in a week. I'm sure she would be..."

"We want to see the islands by sailboat."

"Well, I don't know why. Once you get off the resort property, there's nothing but swampland and mosquitoes. But go ahead and do it your way and see if you don't get a case of malaria or something."

The public has the misconception that all sailors are arrogant yachtsmen who employ a crew of deck hands to keep their ship in shape so the skipper can step aboard on weekends, turn the key and roar off to some quaint little coastal village for an expensive meal and a quiet night away from the city. It just isn't so.

According to a Nielsen survey in 1987, the median income of a sailing household was $63,000. These sailors are by no means poor, but they're not rich either. What they are is the backbone of the American tax system, the "middle class," as it were. If the President and Congress wish to levy a user fee on the boating community, let them provide the benefits as well. They could start by providing a fair and competent Coast Guard whose first priority is protection and assistance to all mariners. Accurate waterway charts that are updated annually by skilled professionals who sound the depths with the latest technology would be another improvement. Give us a sufficient number of pump-out stations in each region so we can comply with the increasingly stringent pollution laws and finally a legal advocate for boaters who have been unfairly evicted from federal waters through the enforcement of unconstitutional ordinances in small coastal communities.

Until the federal government is willing to offer these and other forms of assistance to boaters, they should lay off the taxes. You said we could trust you. You said we could read your lips, but it's beginning to appear that a buck in the hand is worth two in a Bush White House. And I want mine back, George.

SANTA OZ

Dennis Conner might have snatched the America's Cup back from Australia, but the Aussies have something I want even more than the Cup: Christmas.

Oh, sure, we have a Christmas in North America. So does the rest of the world. But our Christmas is cold. Down Under Christmas is hot. Of the two, I prefer theirs. It's no wonder the Aussies walk around saying "g'day" all the time. You'd say "g'day" too if you could spend the holidays sailing in 80 degree weather with a 15 knot wind abeam, sipping a glass of eggnog and singing Christmas carols. It's easy to be friendly and call everyone "mate" when you're warm and tanned and happy.

But their Yuletide tan is not the main source of my envy. It's what the Aussies are doing during the holidays that turn me green. They're sailing! I don't know about you, but the last time I hoisted the mainsail it was up to the attic for winter storage. So lately I've been thinking how nice it would be to have Christmas in the summer. How pleasant would be a New Years sail over to Cape Lookout, or a moonlight cruise up to New Bern as she sparkles in her holiday splendor. There is no question the festivities would be different if Christmas came in the summer, as would some of the Christmas stories we've come to know. Just imagine yourself as a child rocking lightly on a hook in a quiet anchorage. Stars overhead, a hint of cinnamon bread baking in the galley below and your family is gathered in the cockpit on Christmas eve while dad begins to read aloud...

"T'was the night before Christmas down at the Dock House,
Not a patron was stirring, they could not be aroused.

The stockings were hung on the Genny with care,
In hopes that St. Oz would notice the tear.

The children were restless as they lay in their beds,
And complained of the heat and smell from the head.

While I in a tee shirt with mom in my lap,
Had just settled down with a bubbly nightcap.

When out on the water there arose such a clatter,
I sprang from our berth and to see what was the matter.

Away to the foredeck I flew like a flash,
Tripped over a deck cleat and fell with a crash.

A view of the rest of the boats let me know,
We were dragging our anchor onto the fleet down below.

When what to my wandering eyes should appear,
But a self-steering Hinckley sailing up from the rear.

With a little ole skipper adjusting the sheets,
I knew from the odor he had stinky feet.

More rapid than seagulls his crew how they came,
As he whistled and shouted and called them by name.

'Doc Krasher, Wind Dancer, get up here Chris Dickson.
Dis skipper's in trouble, his anchor needs fix'en.'

With a spice island lilt and accent he called,
'Pull dis way, 'n dat way, now let de ding fall.'

As fair weather friends that before the hurricane fly,
When faced with the possibility that all may soon die.

So up to the cockpit came St. Oz and his crew,
With a bag full from Fawcetts and a new Genny too.

His body was tanned from his head to his feet,
And his clothes were lightweight and designed for the heat.

A bundle of goodies he had pulled from his sack,
And he looked for a moment like Panama Jack.

His eyes how they twinkled, like stars in the sky,
And the sun and wind left his lips cracked and dry.

His hair was a mess, like a drift of deep snow,
And a gray stubble beard was beginning to show.

He had a strong face and a muscular build,
But moved with a subtle and graceful skill.

He was coarse and bold, more Jimmy Buffett than elf,
But with the kind of humility I desired in myself.

Catching my eye and nodding his head,
He soon let me know I had nothing to dread.

He spoke not a word, but went straight to his work,
Checking each package like an UPS clerk.

Then returning his bags to the dinghy below,
St. Oz went to visit the other boats in our row.

He moved through the bay, giving presents to all,
And then he was gone like a late summer squall.

But I heard him exclaim as he sailed out of sight,
"Merdy Christmas mon and praise de heavens tonight."

Merry Christmas and happy New Year.

SAILSMANSHIP

Boat shows are a magical time for me. I buy one ticket and go every day and each visit I see something I hadn't seen before. I'm like a small child at a State Fair. You remember how special the fair was when you were a kid? No matter how many times you'd been that year, you always wanted to go again. I became disheartened when I grew older and realized the State Fair wasn't special any longer. It was like a playmate had died.

But I found that playmate again when I went to my first boat show. There I was, picking up every brochure I could find, asking a million questions and leaving more confused than when I'd come. I was certain of only one thing: I wanted a boat and I wanted one bad. I was a window-shopping sailor and the boat show was like Christmas in the mall. I went back every season and looked at the latest version of the same boat I'd seen the year before. Each version was a slight improvement over the previous model, with a few more features in the cabin, more deck space above and more sail area and gear on deck. And always more expensive than the year before.

I never bought anything, mind you. Just looked. The dealers would kind of egg me on, asking if I was going to take the plunge this year. (A clever way to phrase the question, I thought.) And they'd tell me if I'd bought last year, as they'd advised, I could be trading into a larger boat this year. They were right, of course, but all I could do was smile and keep looking. The timing just wasn't right. It was a matter of priorities. There was still the question of finances, kids and careers. But someday, I would tell myself and soon.

It's amazing how long "soon" can be. I look back now and wonder what all the fuss was about. Did I really think my finances would ever get better? Now there's a dream! In relation to income and finances, my family runs a larger deficit than the U.S. Government. Remember Reaganomics and the "trickle down" effect? Remember how we were all going to be better off for it? I got trickled on, all right, but it felt like something other than money.

Kids were another delusion. I pictured my family and myself sailing off to the Bahamas as the fall frost nipped at our heels my son sharing the midnight watch with me as we made that run down to the Abacos. I saw myself teaching him mathematics through celestial navigation, biology along the reefs and foreign languages at exotic ports. Funny thing is, I forgot about friends, grandparents and Little League. Junior doesn't mind if the family sails off to the Bahamas. In fact, he thinks it's a great idea. Wants us to send him a postcard from every port we visit. Nice boy.

About the only thing that has changed to any degree is my career. I'm further down the corporate ladder than when I started, but at least now I don't care. Sailing can have that effect on you. The "movers and shakers" of this world left me behind long ago and the idea of becoming a full-time calypso poet sounds more appealing every day. At least now when I take time off for cruising, there is less income to sacrifice.

Which brings me back to boat shows and why people go. It's not to buy a boat. Heck, you can buy a boat anytime. You don't need a show for that. No, people go for a more important reason. They go to dream. A fascination with boats lies within most of us, no matter if it's a bass boat sitting quietly on a glassy pond or a blue-water cutter slicing through mountainous swells. Boats, big and small, tug at something deep in our heart and offer us that dream all humans desire—the freedom to escape the mundane. The freedom to see life as it was intended, with all its harsh realities and beautiful moments. The freedom to move at our own pace and rise above our sorrows with each swell. Of course, any boat owner will tell you it's all an illusion—just a dream. Owning a boat does offer a kind of freedom, but it also restrains us with its demands on our time and money. Still, there is a certain satisfaction to owning a boat that few possessions can match. Perhaps it's a part of our roots. Our ancestors came to this country in search of freedom and they came by boat. Columbus was looking for new lands, new adventures and he came by boat. We rush through life in newer, faster cars, chasing the green cheese that remains just out of our reach, worried that if we stop, the mob will stomp us flat and leave us behind. Like no generation before us, we live life in the fast lane and sing of slow boats to China.

So this fall I'm off to the sailboat shows again and if the mood strikes and the offers seem too good to resist, I just might buy that big one I've always dreamed of. You only live once, they say and with no guarantee of tomorrow, maybe now is the time to explore the boundaries of this small world from the deck of a proper yacht.

Wherever you're going, that's where you'll be. Set a course for your dream today.

"It's easy to be friendly and call everyone "mate" when you're warm and tanned and happy. I'd say "g'day" too if I could spend Christmas sailing in 80 degree weather with a 15 knot wind abeam while sipping a rum drink and singing Jimmy Buffett's 'Christmas In The Caribbean.'"

Wasting Away, Again in the Carolinas

"I'm going to break out that shaker of salt and whip up a batch of Margaritas - turn up the heat on those shrimp and assemble my friends for a beach bash in Beaufort. Summer's here and I'm wasting away, again in the Carolinas."

THE WINTER OF MY DISCONTENT

Boot Key Harbor, in Marathon, Florida, is the most spectacular anchorage I've never seen. It boasts a protected cove, ample marine facilities, exotic restaurants, lively bars and golden sunsets. It's home to conch fritters, manatees, the seven mile bridge and a host of Jimmy Buffett look-a-likes. There's a colorful little lighthouse at Faro Blanco and cold beer a plenty for the crew. Best of all, you don't have to cross an ocean to get to it. Just take A1A south and follow sun and you won't be disappointed. But I was—or am. You see I've never been.

The difference between going and gone is the difference between lightning and the lightning bug. Nothing can match the electricity you feel when you visit a tropical port for the first time. No amount of reading, dreaming or scheming can replace the actual being there part. You have to sample the island flavors for yourself and it's been almost a year, now, since I announced to anyone who would listen, that I was going to sever the dock lines, cancel my slip, settle the bar tab and head to the Keys. You would think a grown man could load a pocket cruiser on a trailer, hitch it to the car and drive to the sunshine state to unthaw for a few days. It's not like I have to wait on the weather, or crew, or a revised bridge schedule before I can get underway. All I need is a few days from work, someone to help with the driving and the gumption to go. But, therein lies the rub.

You see I can't bring myself to up and leave. I keep telling the wife to have patience. I keep telling her we'll be leaving soon, that there are still a few projects left to complete. The boat needs a new coat of bottom paint and the teak needs cleaning again. I had to slap another coat of varnish on the interior and there's some replacement hardware still on order. You wouldn't want us to go unprepared, would you?

"I don't know why not," she answered. "It's never stopped you before. Don't think I'm not on to your shenanigans. This isn't the first time you've tried to cancel out on me."

"I never…"

"What about the cruise up the Chesapeake?"

"We never caught the right wind."

"Everybody else did."

"They motored."

"So what's wrong with us? Since when did you take a disliking to outboards?"

"They're noisy."

"So are bars, but you've never passed one by."

"We'll go, I promise."

"What about the Bahamas?"

"What about them?"

"We were going to charter a boat and cruise the Abacos."

"The flight to Marsh Harbor was sold out," I protested.

"All of them?"

"We'll go, I tell you, but you have to have patience...like me."

"Patience? I know patience. You've never met the word. What you have is laziness!"

Close. What I have is yellow-bellyness. I'm afraid I'll take a liking to the Keys and refuse to go home. I'm afraid I'll discover the joy of living in a community where the inmates are in charge of the asylum and be tempted to mail my payment book back to the mortgage company. I fear I'll develop a terminal case of the "Keys disease" and plant my hook in a permanent fashion. And if my wife doesn't share my affliction, what then? Today's coward is a hero with a wife, kids and a mortgage. It's for the wife's own good that I don't remove this "C" from my chest or my boat from its slip. I'm guarding the sanctity of our marriage by avoiding one of the unforgivable acts of marriage—abandonment. Since I've never met a temptation I didn't like, love or lust after, it's best I avoid temptation entirely.

The media is full of scoundrels like me who are tripping over our passions in public. Pharisee confessions are the emerging growth stock of the media. "Sin and go public," they say. "The viewers will love it." So I figure if you can't go all the way, what's the point in going at all, which is why I don't go much." This partially explains why I haven't left for Boot Key just yet. I've studied the charts and keep asking myself why I should drive a thousand miles for one week of warmth when I can have the whole winter? I mean, a few days in the Keys won't mean much a month from now when the snow's piling up in the driveway. To expect an underpaid, overworked, boat-bum romantic to be content with a quickie in the tropics is asking too much. I need at least a month settle in. Two months if I'm to find the best bars. A whole winter if they expect me to wear out my welcome.

Ah, but it will never happen. The best I can hope for is a week in the Keys and knowing my luck, it'll take me that long to get the boat off the trailer. Better to just stay in my slip here in Oriental and enjoy my winter of discontent with my friends at Whittaker Creek.

A SELF STUDY IN KEY-WESTERN CIVILIZATION

Adam was the original coastal explorer—a yachting vagabond, if you will. I say this not to challenge the spiritual integrity and claims of infallibility by the fundamentalist friends in my Bible study, but to appease the guilt we boat owners feel for fretting away our working hours with dreams of coastal cruising. I figure if rest and rebellion were good enough for Adam, it's good enough for me. This Biblical oversight has been largely ignored by the do-gooders of our time who claim that the quest for power and self-worship, not leisure was the primary cause of man's fall. It's just a hunch, but I'd say Adam was a land-cuffed sailor, like you and me and he wanted out of the deal.

The struggle for supremacy at any cost is certainly one of humanity's gravest sins, but to lay it all at Adam's feet and claim the lust for lordship did him in, is a bit much. It wasn't the need for power that brought him down. It was the six-day workweek. As proof, I give you Genesis, chapter 2; "And the Lord planted a garden in Eden where He took Adam and put him in the garden to till and keep it. And when He was finished, God rested from all He had done."

So there you have it. While God cruised the emerald waters of the Euphrates River contemplating His next creation, Adam was out pulling weeds from the cucumber plants. You can imagine Adam's frustration. Here was our skipper surrounded by the rivers Pishon, Gihon and Tigris with not so much as a ragged day sailer to be found in the compound. No wonder he quit. What overworked, underpaid, self-respecting sailor wouldn't? I was reflecting on Adam's plight and my own, while sampling a stout round of Pina Coladas at the A&B Marina in Key West. The wife and I had spent a delicious week sailing around Florida's lower Keys, sampling rich Key Lime Pie and strong Cuban coffee. The local variety of conch fritters, though more doughy than those in Man-O-War Cay, had quenched my desire for native cuisine. We'd marveled at the display of wealth from Mel Fisher's "Atocha" and admired the beauty of Key Western architecture. We dined at Margaritaville and learned that Jimmy Buffett does indeed serve the best cheeseburger in the galaxy.

Though warned in advance of the infectious lure of "island time," I'd arrived confident I could resist its power. I'd heard from others that the warm days and mild nights produced an unusual assortment of mutant refugees, but I was certain I wouldn't become one of the defectors. Not me. Not the responsible husband, son and all American dad. People were depending on me to return with a report from paradise—not defect to the deviant culture of America's southernmost outpost.

As I drained the last of my frozen concoction, however, I glanced around with envy at the neighboring craft. Life in Key Western Civilization wasn't too bad. In fact, it was right good. I hinted to the dock master I was interested in some temporary employment and then tallied up my investments and savings, calculating the cash value of my life insurance policy. With leading questions, I learned the expenses of other live aboards and derived a rough cost of living balance sheet. When I went for three days without shaving, I knew the hook was set. I might be down there still, if I hadn't met the crowd of misfits off Christmas Tree Island. This group of ragtag sailors had shucked America's materialistic lifestyle for a more nomadic existence. They had run, quite literally, to the edge of Western Civilization in search of freedom at any price and they were content to live a notch or two beneath the poverty level. These were not the styled images of a slick Madison Avenue ad campaign for Hatteras Yachts. There were no spacious white cruisers—no lobster and beef in the main salon. These were the Fred Sanfords of the cruising community. Their fleet of home built, demasted, waterlogged vessels tainted the anchorage like a festering scab, yet I was glad they were there.

It was comforting to know others had fled the pressures of society and found an aquatic sanctuary. They were statistics from the much maligned "safety net"—a community of dissidents one-step up and two blocks over from the street people of Mallory Square. If this was living down and out in Key West, then free and broke wasn't too bad. But I wanted no part of it. Though the attraction was strong, I have my standards and hot showers and cold drinks are part of them. The desire to come and go, to work and rest, runs deep within me. What fun is paradise if you can't afford to come and go as you like from the compound? Adam found out the hard way. The misfits off Christmas Tree Island saved me from making the same mistake.

So now I'm back home in Oriental where all is right in the world. The days are warm and the nights are cool and the natives are as friendly as ever. The Net House in Beaufort still serves the best Key Lime Pie on the coast and the aroma of Cuban coffee fills our galley in the mornings. My short self-study in Key Western Civilization exorcised the demon of dissatisfaction that prowls around my paradise, but I know he'll return. He never lets me rest for long. But if you find yourself longing for Aegean waters and rustling palms, conch fritters and cold margaritas, I'd recommend you toss aside your pick and ax and tell the big Boss you need some time off to see the rest of His Creation.

Adam would think it only fitting.

A TASTE OF SOME FINE CRUISINE

Last weekend we enjoyed a perfect passage on our sailboat. I know this because I was on board all weekend and sober most of the time and I don't recall anything bad happening. I've seen this sort of thing happen to others, so I guess it was just a matter of time before it nailed us too, but it's a shock just the same. For those who turned to my column this month hoping to find my usual fare of Hard Aground wit and "moronic rambling" you will be pleasantly disappointed, since I have nothing unpleasant to report. To that small, but vocal group that deplores my appearance, attitude, talent and drinking habits, I judge you will find this information gratifying.

What we offer this month is a poor substitute of a sea story—a wholly unworthy imposter of a tidal tale would be more at ease in the winged back chairs of the New York Yacht Club, than beer stained benches of the Dock House patio. Our passage is the simple story of a family that set out on a short passage down the ICW and encountered no difficulties. There were no groundings—no broken engines, or dragging anchors. Instead of blown out headsails, clogged heads and stiff head winds, my family enjoyed one long glorious weekend of rest, relaxation and family bonding. Cruising the way it's meant to be—casual and boring.

It is entirely my fault that we encountered no trouble last weekend. I prepared too well for this trip. I spent an entire winter working on our boat—checking off little projects when they were completed, spending money on repairs when necessary, rebuilding the engine because all of my friends were too lazy to do it for me. In short, I did whatever it took to insure this first trip went well. I had to. It was my last chance to get the family back into sailing. Had this season begun as the last had ended, the family would have abandoned cruising for good and bought a single wide trailer in a swamp along the Waterway, forcing me to retreat to the big sofa on the front lawn to watch other folks sailing south on their boat. Anyway, here's our pleasant story. Try not to fall asleep.

We departed Oriental late Friday afternoon and began plowing into the short chop of the Neuse River. The wind was twenty knots and dead on the nose, but that didn't matter to us, since we were spinning in circles trying to free a crab pot from our swim latter. As we entered the relative shelter of Adams Creek, I began to calculate the remaining distance to Beaufort and realized we would arrive well after dark. I should add that I was aided in this process by a watch, which Bennie thrust in my face just as I was increasing the throttle in hopes of making the next opening at the Core Creek Bridge. She pointed to her watch and the setting sun and just then I realized that we would not make Beaufort that evening. She reminded me that during my years at the Hard Aground Academy of Hard Knots I had learned that thin water and black nights were a lethal combination for a deep draft sailboat, so she dropped the anchor and we elected to spend the night anchored in Cedar Creek. That single decision changed the outcome of our trip.

Early the next morning, we motored to Beaufort. Now here is where it gets really uninteresting, because the engine ran for the entire three hour trip without a single hose springing a leak.

None of the exhaust pipes spewed toxic fumes in the cabin and not one C-clamp rusted through. I don't know why, really. It's just one of those mysteries that will be explained in the after life along with the purpose of the mosquito and avocado.

When we arrived in Beaufort I set two anchors in Taylors Creek, neither of which showed the slightest tendency to drag. We boarded our Avon inflatable and motored over to the dinghy dock to enjoy lunch at Clawson's. That afternoon while Bennie napped, the boys and I played on the beach at Carrot Island. That evening I watched a full moon rise above the low islands of the Core Banks and as the boys slumbered in their bunks, Bennie and I enjoyed each other's company in the cockpit with never a voice raised in panic. In all my years of cruising I cannot recall such a blessed day. We awoke the next morning and found that the Easter Bunny had dropped chocolate bunny butts on the cockpit seat cushions. After our morning devotion, we went window-shopping along Front Street, which is my favorite way to spend money I don't have on things I can't buy. Our return trip to Oriental was just as boring as the trip down to Beaufort, so we spiced it up a little as we entered the Neuse and sailed back to our mooring at Whittaker Creek, picking up the ball on the second try.

Like I said, it was a perfect weekend and makes for dull reading. Now I know there are others who occasionally suffer through a cruise that doesn't go as planned, so I thought you might like to know what I learned from this perfect cruise. After all, I have expounded for so long on how to do it the wrong way that it seems only fitting that I explain what I did right for once.

Step one: Plan early. Four months in advance is about right. Make sure the calendar is clear of all conflicts. If the date you select looks questionable, postpone the trip until you find a date that is suitable to everyone. (That's date, as in day of the month, not new partner in the bunk.) This ingredient is critical. You cannot have a perfect passage if one member of the crew would prefer to be someplace else. In Bennie's case she would prefer to be anywhere other than with me on a boat, but you may have more flexibility in this matter than she does.

Step two: Wait for perfect weather. This may conflict with step one, but you must have gorgeous weather to insure everyone attains his or her comfort level. You would be surprised at how many people go sailing when it is too hot, too cold, too windy or too wet. If step two conflicts with step one, postpone the trip and start all over. I'm sorry, but that's the way it has to be.

Step three: New stuff lasts longer. If you can't afford new parts, sails and boats, find a slip mate who is willing to fix, loan and teach. If you're stuck with an old boat in a marina full of mechanically challenged idiots like myself, move to marina with an active transient population. Most of them will have old boats too, but that's where you'll find the fix, loan and teach crowd.

Step four: When you set off on a weekend cruise, sail with a fleet of friends who know where they're going and stay in the middle of the armada. Do this and you won't get lost or run aground alone. If everyone becomes lost and runs aground on the same shoal, then it's still a beach party and the perfect opportunity to go sand*bar* hopping from boat to boat.

Step five: Don't make firm departure and arrival times. The principal element in any success is flexibility and patience, so hurry up and get both.

Step six: Pack an ample supply of luck and pray a lot. While good luck rarely surprises a man of ability, it's manna from heaven for most of us. If you have a good luck charm, bring it or steal one from someone else.

Step seven: Make the hard decisions yourself. Nothing good ever came out of a committee, so even if your judgment is wrong at least you learned what not to do next time.

Step eight: This is a variation of the "reef early" principal. If you anticipate trouble, prepare for it and don't just wish it away. There is nothing quite as satisfying as slipping on a slicker, shortening the sail and watching it blow a gale as you sit hunkered beneath the dodger with the auto pilot pointing you towards your home port.

Step nine: This is the, "there is no teacher like experience," rule. If you have learned anything new from this column then you should probably be sailing more and reading less.

Bon Voyage Appetite!

GOODY GOODY RAIN DROPS

In ancient days before GPS, IRS and bureaucratic excess ruined boating for low-income sailors, the civilized world had some pretty bizarre ideas about heaven and earth. For one, they reckoned that the sky was as a buffer—a bimini of sorts between man and God which stretched across the cockpit, harbor and most of the Mediterranean islands that weren't yet mentioned on Noah's chart. It was a convenient way of admitting that man didn't know much about God, heaven or the Doppler radar, but they did recognize a good canvas Maker when they saw one. Our feeble understanding of weather has increased considerably since Noah received his first weather report. Today we can track storms from one continent to another, pinpoint from which direction the wind will blow and for how long and in some regions forecasters can even tell when it's going to snow, though in the South we haven't imported that technology yet. Here we still liberate our children from school when it's 33 degrees and raining but incarcerate them again when there is an inch of ice on the road. This idea that the sky acts as a bimini might seem silly now but when you are anchored in a sheltered cove in some far flung chain of islands, miles away from the grimy glow of "mon land" it is easy to look up at the night sky and imagine that there is something big and bright behind all those heavenly holes that twinkle. Logic might suggests that if the sky can hold back all that bright light that is trying to shine through at night then it might also hold back a flood of rain.

Well maybe you wouldn't look at the sky in this way, but I do or did for a while last year when I was invited to study some heavenly holes situated above a Caribbean rain forest. The area I was assigned to investigate was located just a little north of Venezuela and east of Puerto Rico which meant if I was going to sail my boat to that exact location it would take nine months, three outboards and two wives so I decided to fly down and rent a boat instead.

As it turned out, this was my one good idea for the season. I usually make two mistakes and get one good idea a year, so when November rolled around and I'd only made one mistake and hadn't had my good idea, I was feeling a like a dimpled chad on a Palm Beach ballot. The "hole" thing could go either way.

Since I was bound to get a bucket full of lobsters out of the trip, I agreed to skipper the charter boat for this flock of sun-starved women. I wish I could report that my initial research on the relationship between heavenly holes and rain forests revealed a direct link or leak, but that would be a lie and a waste of some well spent research money. Though the sky did drip on a daily basis and provide us with plenty of fresh water showers, it had nothing to due with the heavenly holes or their celestial location.

It turns out the amount of rain and time of the shower depends on how little you want to get wet. The more water your have in your tanks, the more likely it is that you'll get rain. On the other hand, if your tanks are empty and your crew is parched then you can expect a drought of Biblical proportions. Those of you who have been cruising for any length of time already know this, but I was doing research and these findings had to be documented.

Before we sailed for Grenada and our designated tropical rain forest, I had given my crew what I thought was an accurate shower schedule based on certain mathematical calculations. I soon discovered that my formula was slightly skewed since I was using Eastern Standard Time and we were on Eastern Island Time, which is at least one hour ahead or behind our time—I could never decide which. This had the unfortunate effect of rendering all our swim platform showers off by several minutes. Most nights my crew would consume a beer, jump off the swim platform, shed their swimsuits and then stand naked in the dark on the swim platform awaiting their tropical shower rinse. When no rain dripped from the heavenly holes I would turn on our limited supply of stale bilge boat water so the girls could rinse away the soap and salt. Cloaked in Wal-Mart beach towels, my crew of sun-baked beauties would then go below to slip into their standard island issue floral print dresses so I could whisk them ashore in the dinghy where cold beer and hot locals would quench their thirst.

It would be at this point, while we were all waiting for the motor to start, that the heavenly hole would spring a leak and supply us with our first and final rinse of the evening. Soaked, sloshed and suitably dressed for even the most risqué South Beach wet tee shirt contest, I would deposit my crew at the local bar and wish them well, before heading back to the boat to wash away the hardened remains of the day's last lobster hunt. Standing on the swim platform under the deluge of a tropical shower I would bask in the coolness of a rain and wonder why the sky only dripped when the crew was cleaned and dressed.

Near the end of our passage I had an epiphany. For those of you from South Carolina I should explain that an epiphany is not a troupe of string musicians from Monks Corner but rather a pineapple drink laced with lots of rum and a cube of ice. Some say it can also be a sudden revelation, but it's all the same to me. We were anchored behind a sliver of beach contemplating another night of peas and rice, waiting for Paul to deliver his bag of speared fish. We didn't know it at the time but found out later that he had lost the keys to his hatch boards while diving for lobster and was still out by the reef looking for them. (The keys were on a float, but Paul wasn't, which explains why he was found clinging to a pole some hours later fighting a three knot current on an ebbing tide.) My crew was grumbling—gripping actually, about our lack of fine cuisine. I was about to go ashore to investigate the dining possibilities when A.J. suggested the girls go ahead and get in the dinghy.

"I haven't shower yet," Molly protested. "Can't I at least rinse off?"

"Look if it's going to rain let's go ahead, get naked and sit in the dinghy. At least then we'll be near the towels and dry clothes when we get soaked."

"Do you think it's going to rain," Molly asked.

"Do you plan to go ashore?"

"Yes."

"Then it's gonna rain."

And so it did. I've determined that the heavenly holes need a target on which to drip and gray inflatable seems to be the breed of choice. Perhaps an anchorage of Avons resembles raindrops from above and there's a kinetic relationship at work in the heavens. As you can see there is more research to be done on this subject so I've decided to stay a bit longer. Molly thinks we ought to hike to the waterfalls to see if it really rains in a rain forest.

I think it does so I'm going to take a cab, instead.

PLAY IT AGAIN, JIM…IN A LOWER KEY

The splintered blades of the ceiling fan whirled frantically overhead, distributing the heat evenly among the hungry patrons of the Crab Shack. What faint breeze there was, drifted in from the Gulf and through the patio dining area before fleeing down Caroline Street. Crescent shaped sweat stains darkened the red tank top of the hostess as she moved swiftly to seat the anxious group. She removed the dirty dishes, spread a fresh-checkered tablecloth and ushered the party across the room to a table next to ours.

They were the traditional German family, confident and proud, on vacation in the states. The father took his position at the head of the table and with his mother-in-law hunched close to his elbow, translated the menu for her. His wife and younger son discussed the entrees in native tongue, while the older daughter clicked snapshots of the family members.

Like many European women, the young fraulein was of the bra-less society and though it wasn't an issue for her, it became quite an event for the table of young men from Ohio State University.

The French couple had been talking in hushed tones since we'd arrived. They huddled together around a bottle of red wine, licking the sauce from each other's chin when the shrimp missed its target. I had discovered them earlier in the week anchored off Christmas Tree island and had admired the lines of their weathered ketch and now, was captivated by their simple innocence. They were in America and in love and oblivious to all.

I don't know where the cat came from.

Oh, I know it was a descendent of Hemingway's flock and thus, a constant fixture of Key West. But I hadn't noticed him until the German family arrived. From the way "Morris" canvassed the concrete floor, it was apparent he was a regular and seemed to me to have quite a healthy figure for a stray cat. In keeping with feline tradition, however, he remained finicky. He wouldn't eat just any old crumb. It had to be fish. Fresh fish. Preferably the catch of the day. I tried a piece of hush puppy, then French fry. He sniffed, yawned and then ambled on to the other tables. He had all the charm of a tax auditor.

I observed the cat throughout our meal and noticed he was especially fond of the German family. Maybe it was the aroma of the grouper spilling off the table that caught his fancy, or the hope that the young boy might toss him a morsel. For whatever reason, Morris set up camp beneath their table. All was going well until the mother-in-law departed for the restroom.

Morris spied her vacant seat in the cane-back chair and leapt aboard without hesitation. He pawed at the straw cushion until it met with his approval, curled up in a chestnut ball and commenced to take a catnap. The patriarch of the family roared his disapproval to the waitress, who in turn, hurried off to find the manager. The French couple, meanwhile, chastised the old man for disturbing the cat and offered one of their chairs in return, but the proud father would have none of it. The cat was not welcome, period.

The manager appeared and explained the cat was one of many which roamed Key West and was a regular at the Crab Shack. He assured the family that Morris was not a health hazard and would not be a bother. The father was unmoved. He wanted Morris out of the seat. The French couple had garnered additional support for Morris, by now and the whole episode threatened the tranquility of the restaurant. The French, casting a disapproving eye toward the Ohio State boys, argued Morris demonstrated better table manners than many of the patrons. The Germans countered by demanding a peaceful meal in sanitary conditions, without the annoying presence of the cat. The episode was reminiscent of the Cafe American, 1940. All that was missing was Bogie and Bergman. The manager, playing the role of Louie, finally banished Morris from the Crab Shack and calm was restored, but I sensed, Louie's efforts were strictly for show. After all, Hemingway's cats have ruled the streets of Key West for decades. They are a permanent fixture of the Key

Western architecture and certainly more accepted by the locals than the tourist.

The incident served to highlight how tourism has tarnished these islands in the stream.

Make no mistake about it. Key West has gone big time and everyone wants a slice of the Key Lime Pie. In the spring, college students flee to her tropical shores in record numbers and the sounds of youth reverberate from Sloppy Joe's well into the night. Nowadays, if you want to go crazy on Caroline Street, you have to take a number and stand in line. This new influx of money has been a boon for T-shirt vendors, restaurants, bars and most recently, the sailboat charter business. The latest trend in cheap vacations is to rent a 40-foot Irwin, cram eight kids aboard and party all week. It sure beats the parking lot view of the Econolodge.

International travelers have discovered Key West's rustic charm, as well. Europeans and Asians arrive on the weekly cruise ship or drive down from Disney World, intoxicated by the lure of "Margaritaville." Certainly, the merchants don't seem to mind the business, although, you get the feeling the locals are getting tired of all this attention. In fact, you have to hunt pretty hard to find a native "conch." You might think the residents would get disgusted with the crowds and move to one of the other keys. Some have, but the majority remain in Key West because it is still the last outpost for bums and romantics.

Stroll down her streets on a summer's evening when the crowds are gone and the air is electric with thunderstorms and you begin to understand why so many artists and poets have come to call Key West their home. There are nights when you can look out across the Gulf Stream on the moonlit water and hear the diesel hum of shrimp boats probing the bottom for those tender critters. This fragile rock glistens at the end of the island chain like an uncut diamond, refusing to be shaped into the mold of other tourist cities. Progress has won a few, to be sure, but the conflict is one of guerrilla warfare and the natives are at home in the mangroves.

Still, you have to wonder what Hemingway would think of this new Key West. He would probably consider it too gaudy and cheap and he would be right. He would ridicule her lurid behavior in his best-selling manner and condemn the settlement as a cheap imitation of itself. Then he would purchase a small home on one of the side streets and blend into the architecture, for that is the magic of Key West. Even when she is bad, she is better than most. And as long as Hemingway and his cats were both welcomed at the Crab Shack, he would not think Margaritaville such a bad place to live out one's fantasies.

So, break out the charts and forward the mail. Restock the icebox and turn up the tunes. It's time to play it again, Jimmy…in a lower Key.

WASTING AWAY AGAIN IN THE CAROLINAS

The sign on Broad Street still reads Oriental, but it might as well read, Marathon, Nassau, Marsh Harbor or Roadtown. The days are warm, the winds robust and the indigo water peppered with white canvas sails. This is the season for bawdy songs, chilled Becks in the cockpit and lazy afternoons at the helm—fresh shrimp and seasoned conversation around the anchorage. They are the Jimmy Buffett days...and I love'em!

Some people spend all their life searching for paradise and never find it. But then, some never sail the Pamlico Sound on a September afternoon or stroll the Beaufort waterfront at dusk. A number of sailors I know spend their good time and money motoring up and down the Intracoastal Waterway on their way to more exotic locations and never stop to admire the azaleas in Wilmington or the charm of Old Charleston. If all this sounds like a Department of Tourism publication for the Carolinas, I apologize. It's just that I've reacquainted myself with an old friend and fallen in love again.

I didn't mean to. In fact, I wasn't aware I had strayed at all, but I had for my mind had wandered and that's sin enough for me. It began with little indiscretions. To increase the magazine's coverage, I told myself I should move my boat to Key West, where the days are warm and the nights are gay and unemployment seems to be a coveted status symbol. A few months later I considered a cruise over to the Abacos to cover the winter sailing scene. Cheap airfare was the lure and Hopetown in January was the silver glint of the hidden barb. During my weaker moments, I caressed the fantasy of exploring the Virgin Islands, the West Indies and beyond. Fortunately, a company of stout warriors from the Becks Brigade usually knocked me out before I could act and thus, disaster was averted.

Then last September I awoke to find myself at the end of the rainbow. The sun rose over the Outer Banks, spilling its quick-silver rays across South River and a crisp, breeze gathered the fragrance of cedar and sprinkled it generously around the anchorage. The harbor was the temperature of warm bath water and I treated myself to one, while a lone brown pelican shared the remains of my bagel and strawberries. It suddenly occurred to me that I'd been running up the rainbow from the wrong end. All my dreaming of paradise had brought me home.

Some might argue the winters in the Carolinas are too cold and therefore rate it low on the paradise scale. I'll admit, it does get a might unpleasant at times, but no place is perfect. Not even the islands. The coldest vacation I've ever squandered was two weeks in the Bahamas when a cold front grabbed lower Florida by it's orange clusters and the wind chill plunged to an ominous 40 degrees in Hopetown. Because we were in the "tropics" and weren't prepared for the cold evenings, we wrapped ourselves in skimpy beach towels and hearty shots of Captain Morgan's dark rum and prayed the propane stove would last through the night. The only sunburn received was a pair of singed eyebrows from standing too close to the burner.

If extensive facilities and plenty of sunshine is your idea of para-dise, they say Florida is the place to go. I did, but it wasn't—at least, not for me. They have facilities all right—with a price to match. If you thought you might anchor out to cut the cost, think again. Many of Florida's prime anchorages limit your stay to a couple of days per month and if you defy the regulation, they'll seize your vessel. It's all illegal, of course, but the government officials elected with condo dweller dollars are controlled by a legion of lawyers to insure these discriminating ordinances are enforced. As for the sunshine, it doesn't. At least not as often as they say it does. And who is this "they" anyway? It's them that's been there and left because they got tired of being treated like second-class citizens. "They" are trying to get us to go "there" so "they" can have our space "here."

The Virgin Islands make the paradise hit parade with a lot of sailors and rightly so. It is true the more popular cruising areas are becoming commercialized and congested with pale invaders, but there is the still an opportunity for a shrewd romantic to discover his tropical Eden provided he has the time and money—which I don't. So what is left? Where does a body go to find peace and solitude—warmth and wind? I could try Mexico or the South Pacific, but I don't speak the language. There's always Australia and New Zealand, but they're half way around the world and I'd want to visit my family more than once a year. Perhaps I should try the Mediterranean, Europe or the Orient? I mean I gotta go somewhere. Isn't that the whole idea of cruising—to explore exotic locations? Isn't that why we buy more boat than we need and pay for dockage space in deep harbors when we'd be just as well off with a shoal draft vessel in a narrow creek? Someday we're gonna quit our job. Some day we're gonna run away. Someday we're gonna sail to paradise.

But for now, I'm going to break out that shaker of salt and whip up a batch of Margaritas—turn up the heat on those shrimp and assemble my summer friends for a little Beaufort beach bash. Summer's here...and I'm wasting away again in the Carolinas.

978-0-982-20650-8

Made in the USA
Middletown, DE
16 June 2016